MW00810846

High Impact Practices with Urban
Youth—Circles at the Center

HIGH IMPACT PRACTICES WITH URBAN YOUTH— CIRCLES AT THE CENTER

A Guidebook for Practitioners and Scholar-Activists

Yan Dominic Searcy and Troy Harden

OXFORD
UNIVERSITY PRESS

Oxford University Press is a department of the University of Oxford. It furthers
the University's objective of excellence in research, scholarship, and education
by publishing worldwide. Oxford is a registered trade mark of Oxford University
Press in the UK and certain other countries.

Published in the United States of America by Oxford University Press
198 Madison Avenue, New York, NY 10016, United States of America.

Library of Congress Cataloging-in-Publication Data
Names: Searcy, Yan Dominic, editor. | Harden, Troy, editor.
Title: High impact practices with urban youth—circles at the center : a guidebook for
practitioners and scholar-activists / [edited by] Yan Dominic Searcy and Troy Harden.
Description: New York, NY : Oxford University Press, [2023] |
Includes bibliographical references and index.
Identifiers: LCCN 2023013827 (print) | LCCN 2023013828 (ebook) |
ISBN 9780197549926 (hardback) | ISBN 9780197549940 (epub) |
ISBN 9780197549957
Subjects: LCSH: Urban youth—Education—United States. |
Urban youth—Services for—United States. | Group work in education—United States. |
Social group work—United States.
Classification: LCC LC5141 .H56 2023 (print) | LCC LC5141 (ebook) |
DDC 370.9173/20973—dc23/eng/20230614
LC record available at https://lccn.loc.gov/2023013827
LC ebook record available at https://lccn.loc.gov/2023013828

DOI: 10.1093/oso/9780197549926.001.0001

Printed by Sheridan Books, Inc., United States of America

CONTENTS

INTRODUCTION

A FIRST LESSON FROM THE CIRCLE

The interior of the high school was a cruel April fool's joke. The outside bragged manicured landscaping and a sturdy, three-story exterior supported with a sextet of limestone Greek columns that simultaneously nodded in three directions—the city's celebration of ancient wisdom, the prosperity of the early twentieth century, and the promise of the future. But inside captured what is wrong with many urban high schools: poorly maintained cinder block–walled hallways and classrooms that tilted toward a correctional facility more so than an instructional facility. There were guards on every floor, a roving police officer, metal detectors at the entrance, and analog loudspeakers crackling orders to students.

Getting official clearance to begin our grant-funded work with youth, the newly appointed grant program director and I were there to begin to recruit students. We walked into the high school library to meet one of the school counselors, who we were told would assist us with connecting to students for our program, which aimed to improve health outcomes for urban youth. Once inside, we found the library to be a gathering place for students interested in great conversations rather than great books. To the students, we most likely looked like the latest float in the usual parade of suit-clad observers. The program director and I were approached by a student who probed matter-of-factly: "What are you here for?" I explained the program and that we wanted to recruit sophomores. He then countered with skepticism: "You trying to get students how?" I answered that we were getting the help of a guidance counselor. He replied: "Oh no that will never work." As a senior he said he couldn't participate but shared his opinion on the best approach to get sophomores. Recognizing his knowledge, I asked if he would be willing to assist with recruiting. Soon after his yes, we introduced Dennis to the circle.

High Impact Practices with Urban Youth—Circles at the Center. Yan Dominic Searcy and Troy Harden, Oxford University Press. © Oxford University Press 2023. DOI: 10.1093/oso/9780197549926.001.0001

Within 11 years, Dennis had appeared as a panelist on national television multiple times, finished a bachelor's degree in political science, completed a master's degree from one of the nation's premier programs in urban planning, and recently gained his doctorate in educational leadership. This is the same person who moved multiple times throughout his youth, had few positive role models, endured the relational trauma of having a brother hospitalized with multiple gunshot wounds, and grew to manhood in the violence of Chicago. This is also the same urban youth whose college entrance exam score predicted his failure.

High impact practices (HIPs) were essential to his success. Those HIPs are detailed in the following pages.

We begin each chapter with a brief narrative, "Lessons from the Circle," reflective of our interactions with youth or program staff that are germane to an HIP. We frame circles within the context of youth group work and clarify our use of circles as an HIP. These circles, we argue, are a critical component of all the HIPs explored in the book.

The narratives serve as an introduction to important themes for those new to urban youth work, and they serve as an examination of the familiar to those currently working directly with urban youth. Stories, we find, supply a conceptual framework from which to explore HIPs. Stories reflect, capture, and compel.

FRAMING THE BOOK AND FRAMING THE WORK

Books on youth work tend toward several groupings: textbooks for students, scholarly research on interventions, and curriculum for practitioners. This book was written to bridge the gap between practitioners and researchers who are specifically working to improve the life outcomes of urban youth. This is a guidebook best thought of as a way to frame interventions. We do not offer a specific curriculum. We do, however, offer approaches to building a curriculum around content and share insight on *how* to engage youth in a curriculum.

This book is to assist front-line practitioners and program directors. This book is reflective of a combined over five decades of work with urban youth. Skilled, informed caring is imperative in order to improve youth outcomes. We know that caring is really not enough. Our approach to youth work has not been captured in the existing literature, and we wanted to share the lessons we learned to assist with impacting the interventions of others working with youth.

Our programmatic work has primarily been involved with improving outcomes for at-risk urban youth. Here, however, we resist the label of at-risk because we acknowledge that all urban youth are essentially "at risk" for engaging in behavior that has consequences for criminal justice system involvement, low educational attainment, sexually transmitted diseases, unintended pregnancies, accidents and behaviors that lead to severe impairment or death, substance abuse, and mental health concerns. We also resist the label of "at promise" for the same reasons. We acknowledge that all urban youth are at promise.

Urban as a descriptor carries with it a connotation derived from marketing companies as a euphemism for people who are Black and Latino. Our use of urban is not defined by racial characteristics but rather environmental characteristics—residing in a city with a population over 50,000 as defined by the U.S. Census Bureau. Racial and ethnic diversity abound in urban areas, and HIPs necessitate cultural humility (Yeager and Bauer-Wu 2013). Influenced by prior research, Yeager and Bauer define cultural humility as a process involving self-reflection and critical examination of one's own cultural identities and beliefs while learning about other cultures. Cultural humility also acknowledges that culture is dynamic and competency can only be approximated and never fully realized. Attending to and embedding cultural dynamics in program approaches is requisite and reflective of HIPs. We stress, however, that facilitator authenticity and personal humility are critical components to working with youth.

A note here is that the term *of color* is not used in our writing. This term is a political term "that allows for a more complex set of identity for the individual—a relational one that is in constant flux" and is a term "that attempts to show the humanity rather than a social identity or condition" (Malesky 2014; Hampton 2019). The term *of color* is positioned in such a way to be affirmative rather than pejorative. We acknowledge person of color as a political term but note that it is a problematic term that minoritizes the global numeric majority of those who are considered persons of color. We have consciously chosen to discard the practice of promoting an erroneous assumption that the *exceptions* are "people of color" and that the minority are "people of color." We are discussing Black, Latino, Asian, and Indigenous people unless otherwise clarified.

The book is organized around HIP-influenced program design. It originates from a theory base the authors suggest is how youth development is best understood and how that understanding leads to approaches to engage youth. That theory base, which is grounded in the person-in-environment (PIE) perspective, underscores the intersection of history;

social structures (economic, racial, gendered, sexual, and political); and how those impact behavior and potential life outcomes.

The chapters are organized around a program planning format. We move from theory to program form to recruitment strategies, then to practices aimed to solidify participation and produce positive outcomes to those strategies aimed to reinforce program impacts. Our aim is to be practical and tactical.

Studies abound related to program analysis, curricular assessments, and program outcomes. However, the evidence of effective *methods* is not well translated to practitioners. At a minimum, those with formal education are grounded in youth and human development theoretical perspectives and in social work generalist practice incorporating the PIE theoretical perspective, which views that human behavior is a function of the interaction between the person and his or her social environment. Those practitioners without formal education are often left to their own devices to "hit or miss" and "trial and error" concerning working with youth.

As many programs are encouraged to utilize the latest evidence-based practices (EBPs), often coinciding with grant-funding cycles, organizations and programs run the danger of "innovation overkill," where skeptical providers simply employ the language that funders want to hear while *practice* remains largely unaddressed. Undergraduate and graduate social work practice courses that focus on youth and adolescent development, mentoring, evidence-informed practices, practice courses for work in schools, community, and social service settings will find perspective here. Although focused on urban youth, what is shared has implications for other demographics and practice areas.

CHAPTER LAYOUT

Chapter 1 begins by identifying and defining HIPs. It discusses the development of our work with young people. We share the stories and data behind the programs that reflect HIPs with urban youth. We include a specific discussion of circles. In this section, we trace the origins of circles to indigenous cultures and their use to address conflict, promote equity, and enhance individual contribution in a group setting. We also frame circles within the context of group work and clarify our use of circles as a HIP form of group work. These circles, we argue, are a critical component of all the HIPs explored in the book.

Chapter 2 engages the theories behind our approaches with youth. Attention is placed on the social work PIE theoretical approach. The chapter also engages the theoretical perspective that frames the use of circles and contextualizes youth flourishing as a programmatic goal.

Chapter 3 focuses on the important process of selecting a leader for program development, including the characteristics that youth program managers embody. Although much has been written about management and leadership within the human service context, less is written about these characteristics, skills, knowledge, and values of youth development leaders. The chapter explores the concept of authentic leadership and then moves to explore the characteristics and leadership traits of successful of youth development leaders. Those traits include authenticity, inclusiveness, availability, care, and accountability.

Chapters 4 and 5 provide discussion of the practical application of HIP tools. Chapter 4 covers recruitment, retention, and participation. Considered as both art and science, the focus of the chapter is on recruitment. Transportation, safety getting to programming sites, and the actual program sites are also considered as key elements for improving retention and participation. Additionally, the chapter discusses the importance of considering youth personality attributes.

After exploring some of our work with recruitment, retention, and ongoing participation, Chapter 5 covers the operational dynamics of discussion circles. As the center of HIPs, we detail the mechanics of circle management. The chapter explicitly discusses how to convene the circle, set ground rules for participation, set meeting agendas, and manage the emotional safety of the circle.

In Chapter 6, we explore curriculum development through incorporation of EBPs. The chapter provides details of curriculum development based on EBPs, practitioner attributes, desired program outcomes, and utilizing program moments to achieve high impact.

Chapter 7 explores youth leadership, including creating spaces where young people can both be themselves and open themselves for challenge and transformation. We believe that the core of youth work is offering young people a chance to demonstrate skill and knowledge, and that young people thrive in working alongside caring and creative adults. Leadership-framed programs provide opportunities for youth to demonstrate skill, knowledge, and purpose. Covering formal and informal program leadership opportunities, we separate leadership into the categories of contributional leadership (planning and management) and representational leadership (autonomous self-determination).

Chapter 8 establishes the importance of including retreats as part of youth programming. The chapter focuses primarily on retreat planning and identifies and discusses 10 elements to include when planning for youth retreats.

Chapter 9 covers the importance of participant recognition and celebrations as ways to increase participation, collaboration, self-esteem, and short-term impact. Attention is given to how celebrations can be structured to maximize program impact on youth. Chapter 10 focuses on follow-up as a means to buttress sustained, long-term impacts. The chapter expands the idea of follow-up to include in-program preparation for youth transitions out of programming. We conclude the book with an epilogue that addresses the inherent challenges of behavioral change but lands on the encouraging potential in circles.

CHAPTER 1

An Introduction to High Impact Practices

Lesson from the Circle

"Remember, you can't transfer relationships." The admonition came from Kenny Ruiz, who had been working with gang-involved and at-risk youth for two decades. He often shared that just because you show up and have worked with youth in the past means nothing at the start of a new program. Each relationship is unique, and each new relationship with a youth requires development. He lamented that just because he knows a youth doesn't mean his introduction of them to us means anything to them.

Gathered in our own circle, we prepared for the 6-month program that would be bringing together youth from varying racial and ethnic groups and neighborhoods. Kenny admonished that we have to open the program big. That last admonition rings like a retail business owner talking about a grand opening to generate excitement.

In the planning circle were over 200 years of collected experience. Two of us were previously gang involved and formerly incarcerated and were neophytes to youth work. Two of us were scholars with years of community experience. Two of us were long-time community youth program directors. One of us was previously incarcerated and formerly gang involved, but who had been working many years at the community center where we were to host the program.

Our own circle intended to solidify team relationships, build trust, model the circles that would be the center of our program, and explore through self-examination our own socioemotional dynamics that may impact the upcoming work. We worked out the elements of the program; we addressed respective roles in the program and talked about program goals. This, we found, set the tone for the rest of the program. But why? By modeling the circle in our planning, it allowed us to understand the dynamics the youth would experience.

High Impact Practices with Urban Youth—Circles at the Center. Yan Dominic Searcy and Troy Harden, Oxford University Press. © Oxford University Press 2023. DOI: 10.1093/oso/9780197549926.003.0001

It also sensitized us to the emotions (anxiety, unsurety, nervousness, fear, vulnerability) that the youth may experience so we could attend to it in the program.

We did open big. About 40 youth attended (mainly Mexican, Puerto Rican, and Black). Transportation was arranged to bring the neighborhoods together. A circle was convened and an active bingo ice breaker got the youth to interact. We closed not knowing how many youth would return to the program the following week, but we closed knowing that what we did had impact. We demonstrated the following: A group of caring adults had formed as a resource; there were people available in the community whether they asked them or not; there was a safe physical space available for activity; and youth would be partners and not told they were the problem.

WHAT ARE HIGH IMPACT PRACTICES?

High impact practices (HIPs) are evidence-based educational practices that have been shown to "deepen student learning and engagement, and raise levels of performance, retention and success for students" (Kuh 2008). While the term *high impact practices* enjoys frequent use in higher education related to promoting practices that improve student learning outcomes, retention, and graduation rates, we appropriate the term to apply to evidence-based practices (EBPs) that are shown to increase program participation and increase the likelihood of meeting program designated outcomes and decrease negative risk-taking behavior among urban youth. HIPs also reflect the higher education dynamics of increasing program participation and retention rates.

Higher education HIPs include

- First-year seminars and experiences
- Common intellectual experiences
- Learning communities
- Writing-intensive courses
- Collaborative assignments and projects
- Undergraduate research
- Diversity/global learning
- Service learning, community-based learning
- Internships
- Capstone courses and projects

The HIPs are linked to increasing program participation because they increase a sense of belonging (Strayhorn 2019). Miller et al. (2018) noted that with participation, engagement with faculty increases a sense of belonging. This increased sense leads to more program participation. Belonging, in effect, moves participants from a status of subject to agent. Agency leads to program ownership. As a result, it is not that youth are compelled to comply to attend programming from an outside source; they are compelled to attend due to an internalized sense of ownership where they can see the impact of their participation. That is, they are not objects to be changed but agents of the change process. The factors that influence why HIPs are successful with college students, increasing retention and meeting program outcomes, are the reasons to employ them with youth work.

A note is that advances in neuroscience concerning understanding adolescent brain development, trauma-informed approaches, and youth leadership tools can be incorporated in programming with HIPs to create meaningful development experiences for young people. We argue that it matters more about how the participants *feel* about the program and the people running the program than it does about a particular curriculum.

Program participation and engagement are motivated by a sense of ownership, agency, affirmation of self; exploration of self; attaining useful skills, independence, and relationships that are supportive, affirming, and safe. To be clear, HIPs allow for self-exploration. They create an environment that allows for risk taking and exploration with minimal judgment, high levels of encouragement, and also extra program support. That is, there is still a sense that the program is "in session" even outside of regular programming or business hours.

We identify HIPs with urban youth to include

- Circles
- Program team building
- Recruitment, retention, and participation
- Processes to create participant cohesion
- Crafting content before curriculum
- Embedded mentoring
- Fostering youth leadership
- Retreats
- Celebrations
- Post-program follow-up

The following chapters will detail these program HIPs and why circles are the foundation for them. But here in this first chapter, we cover what makes HIPs high impact.

We offer an initial caution. Fundamentally, youth work is difficult to assess because youth behavioral change frequently occurs incrementally. Youth often do not change overnight. While HIPs are largely assessed on a short-term programmatic basis, we are careful to note that they are directed toward long-term, sustained, positive transformational impacts. Impact should not be confounded with immediacy.

One critical reason why HIPs have impact is because they involve creating an environment where youth have ownership of the program. Ownership has been written about across youth literature. We do not want to marginalize this as simply a youth concept. Ownership within commerce and community reveals that the concept embeds feelings of pride and agency. Ownership tends to orient behavior positively toward the object that is owned. Likely more profound, however, is what occurs when there is no ownership or assessment that there is no future possibility of ownership.

There will be behavior to seek autonomy to own something or seeking opportunity to own. There will be resistance to participation in those areas where there is no ownership or ownership possibility. There likely will be the creation of spaces or institutions to own. There will likely be attempts to damage the spaces where there is an absence of ownership. Graffiti is an example of attempting to establish ownership. Tagging, putting one's name on an item, is an example. In the eyes of the person or institution that receives the tag, it is defacing property. In the eyes of the person tagging, it is asserting ownership. It is also affirming presence in an area or a society where taggers are considered invisible or do not see themselves.

One can argue, then, that youth spaces where youth do not see themselves (as owners) will result in resistance and even behavior that seeks to damage those spaces. This can be seen in neighborhoods, schools, and, of course, youth programs. Where youth see themselves as owners is essential. Providing opportunities for program ownership among participants has high impact.

OWNERSHIP

Harano (2017) writes:

> The relationship between designers and recipients of design often reproduces privilege and oppression by positioning the former as experts and the latter

as "problems" to solve. The exclusion of young people in curricular design for summer programming highlights this sentiment; the public, private, and social sectors often view young people, especially low-income youth of color in large cities, as "risks" in need of solutions, like summer employment.

Ownership is often related to youth voice being expressed, heard, and incorporated into programs (Mantooth and Hamilton 2004). Ownership is also reflected in youth having decision-making power related to activities (Cater et al. 2013). "From a psychological theoretical perspective, youth voice is grounded within the need for autonomy, one of three basic needs described by cognitive evaluation theory, a sub-theory of self-determination theory (Ryan and Deci 2000). Cognitive evaluation theory describes social and environmental factors that lead to higher levels of intrinsic motivation. In its simplest form, intrinsic motivation is conceptualized as a drive to learn because of the joy and challenge that is engendered in the individual, whereas extrinsic motivation involves external forces motivating a person to perform or engage for some external reward or outcome." Intrinsic motivation is cultivated through providing ownership opportunities for youth program participants. Providing opportunities for intrinsic motivation leads to the likelihood of greater youth engagement in programs.

Linnenbrink and Pintrich (2003) posit that engagement in formal education activities is largely about those behaviors that can be measured or observed, such as seeking assistance when challenges emerge, amount of time spent on learning tasks, as well as persistence. The authors also add that for youth development that engagement is essentially the same—behavioral. When youth are actively engaged in programming as owners and have volition in programming, a reciprocal process occurs. Program participation provides affirmation of youth input and shows that their opinions have value. As a result of affirmation, youth participation continues. In settings where youth often do not see themselves as having the ability to show ownership or see the impacts of their contributions, program participation is not likely to continue unless compelled. To increase the likelihood of positive program outcomes, it is imperative to include opportunities for youth to engage in program planning.

Youth involvement in program planning does not need to be initially in program proposals as it may be unknown who specific participants will be. However, involvement should be embedded once the community of participants is identified. That is, while a program idea may be put forward, the program itself should have places where participants can determine direction. For example, a program may choose to have a series of field trips. Embedding ownership is allowing participants to determine where the field trips will be. Additionally, students may assist in the crafting of the agenda of the field trips.

AGENCY

Agency is a learning sciences construct that has multiple definitions. Throughout this book we incorporate a multidisciplinary and culturally grounded approach, utilized by Barton and Tan (2010), who describe agency as follows: "At once the possibility of imagining and asserting a new self in a figured world at the same time it is about using one's identity to imagine a new world and different world." Agency is operationalized here as the activity of doing and contributing to a project or a discussion. Agency ultimately makes youth contributions visible. Agency, we argue, is related to ownership and also has positive self-esteem impacts. Larson and Angus (2011) state: "Development of agency, almost by definition, requires youth to be intentional producers of their own development." The authors identify agency skills as "cognitive tools, including insights, precepts, knowledge, and action schemas that youth might employ to help them achieve goals." They add that adolescence is the period when complex reasoning skills emerge. Agency during adolescence, as many youth workers posit, is a process whereby youth can develop their "superpowers." Agency gains particular import as there are limited opportunities for formal recognition of inventiveness in "constraining environments" (Barton and Tan 2010).

Agency coupled with positive interactions with program staff echo what was shared previously that how participants feel about a program is more important than the curriculum. Krauss et al. (2014) note that youth and adult partnerships have influence, "not simply because youth have authentic opportunities to participate in decision making forums, but equally important, because the young people are recognized and cared for by adults with in." Developmentally, the partnerships that reflect youth agency "[have] emerged as a key practice for enacting two features of effective developmental settings: supportive adult relationships and support for efficacy and mattering" (Krauss et al. 2014).

CIRCLES AT THE CENTER

The circle is the HIP that is the centering component for all youth programming. Our research across several programs links discussion circles to positive youth outcomes and thus places it at the center of HIPs. Discussion circles are effective tools for planning and cohesion. Circles provide a venue for communication, emotional support and healing, encourage problem-solving and creativity, and promote a "sense of shared purpose" (Boyes-Watson 2005). Circles are also reflective of client-centered approaches that have been linked to positive outcomes for at-risk youth.

Over the past two decades, circles have gained greater international notoriety particularly as a tool for conflict resolution through peace circles. However, circles can address trauma, promote healing, enhance communication, and even be a tool to facilitate meetings.

Though seemingly a new age approach to addressing modern social problems, it is not new. Circles derive from thousand-year-old practices of indigenous people (Boyes-Watson 2005; Smith 2003; Pranis et al. 2003). Sometimes called peace circles, healing circles, or talking circles, the more recent history is tied to North American Native Americans, quite specifically the Lakota Sioux ethnic group's *hocokah* (Mehl-Madrona and Mainguy (2014).

Clearly, circles are not represented only in North American indigenous ethnic groups. Variations of the circle exist across South America, Asia, and Africa (Dioum Kelly 2016). One such variation is the practice of the Dogon in western Africa, where adult males gather in the togu na. The togu na is a structure with a low roof that prevents standing. The low roof is intentional to prevent physical conflict when discussing contentious issues. It acts on the idea that it is difficult to fight when it is impossible to stand. The circle's genesis derives from indigenous populations from varying continents who utilized it for resolving conflicts, collective planning, and maintaining community.

As we engage the use of circles, we also are sensitive to that which is presented by indigenous scholars such as Smith (2012) and Wilson (2008), who argue that there must be expressions of debt to and acknowledgment of the appropriation of practices to serve colonial/imperial practices that often led to the reasons for the problems (Kovach 2009). To be certain, we acknowledge that Western cultural values have created structures and institutions that value property rights and control over human rights and harmony.

We turn to an indigenous practice cleaved from the very cultures that have been the victims of genocide to look for solutions to the problems that their elimination and adoption of Western values led to. We acknowledge that we are using indigenous practices to solve the problems caused by the imposition of Western colonial practices that essentially destroyed those practices along with a way of life.

CIRCLES VERSUS GROUP WORK

Circles are a form of group work. Group work is one of the three signature practice modalities within the social work profession. Defined in the *Encyclopedia of Social Work*, group work is "Goal-directed activity that brings together people for a common purpose or goal" (Toseland and Horton 2013). Though derived from a history of social action, group work evolved into two distinct categories: treatment related and task oriented. Treatment focuses on addressing the behavioral deficits of the individual within the context of a group dynamic. Through establishing a sense of commonality, treatment groups provide support, shared experience, increased motivation, and promotion of decreasing personal denial to assist in addressing behavioral deficits (Levine and Gallogly 1985). Task groups often focus on achieving predetermined goals or are organized to set goals. Task group goals may not have an individual focus on change or be therapeutic in nature but tend toward a collective movement toward attaining a goal or completing a task (Levine and Gallogly 1985). These tasks may be client, community, or organizationally oriented.

Circles are used in both categories of group work involving a treatment orientation and a task orientation. However, the circles work that is our focus can be categorized as task oriented. Circle-based programming is intended to improve behavioral outcomes—tasks. Those tasks can be developmental or community-related tasks. Boyes-Watson (2005) defines the circle as a process and a "method for youth development, community organizing, emotional healing, conflict resolution, political dialogue, team building, collaboration, and organizational planning."

Circles are HIPs reflective of achievement of behavioral tasks and are examples of an EBP due to their link to positive results such as violence prevention among youth (Backer and Guerra 2011). Research shows that circles are linked to promoting positive youth development through offering a safe environment composed of caring adults and supportive peers that provide positive life skill-building opportunities.

Our application of circles in multiple settings and with various program purposes confirms the results of prior research that circles promote positive youth development. We incorporate Backer and Guerra's (2011) suggestion to be proactive in promoting adaptation of circles to ensure success for programs targeting urban youth. Circles are at the center of effective youth programming.

We clarify that circles, when implemented well, can overcome Backer and Guerra's (2011) contention that successful implementation of EBPs does not last. Greenwood (2010) note implementation of EBPs is not particularly widespread. We overcome, by providing specific discussion of the HIP's elements of circles, what Greenwood (2010) cautions as the confusion over what to include in programming due to many EBPs being identified through "non-rigorous standards."

Circles communicate egalitarianism by physical layout of the circle and are juxtaposed with other physical layouts experienced by youth, which tend to reinforce their status as minors and having limited power. Vis-à-vis a courtroom or a classroom, the circle visually and physically presents an egalitarian space. We concur with: "The real force comes from the values embodied by the circle. These values lay beneath the surface and are practiced through the structure and rituals of the circle itself."

CHAPTER 2

Theory Informing Practices

Lesson from the Circle

On the last day as the program director arrived, the office was emptied and readied for the next director. It was an anticlimactic day without farewell festivities. No cake. No party. The program served pregnant and parenting female youth. The 24-hour program was structured as an intergenerational model pairing actual grandmothers with young mothers to provide supervision and prepare them to ultimately live independently. A case manager and administrative assistant rounded out the staff.

The circle was utilized in the weekly life skills component of the program. As an element of the program, "consequences" were given for varying program infractions. The consequences ranged from curfew to financial impacts as program allowances would be fined. The residents could earn the allowances back by completing community service. The excitement with the director leaving was that residents believed that their accumulated fines would be delivered to them on my last day. They were incorrect.

Four o'clock struck, and while I wrapped up a conversation with the case manager and administrative assistant, a resident came to the office and asked for her program allowance money. I shared that it would not be released, and she would have to talk to the incoming program manager. At that she launched into an expletive-laden rage: "Ooooh, I will fuck you up!" shared many times. She charged toward me at the now-empty desk. The case worker rose to meet her charge and held her from getting close enough to throw punches. I inched from the side of the desk and eased by the enraged resident, who was yelling and pulling away from the case manager.

Almost 18 years later, the case manager and the former resident and I still laugh at that program memory. The former resident and I talk several times a year. She tells me that she was seething mad, and I should have given her the money and she really did want to hurt me. After retiring from traveling

High Impact Practices with Urban Youth—Circles at the Center. Yan Dominic Searcy and Troy Harden,
Oxford University Press. © Oxford University Press 2023. DOI: 10.1093/oso/9780197549926.003.0002

the world with the U.S. Navy, starting her own business, completing college degrees, and having her daughter begin college, the former resident is beginning a new postmilitary career—teaching youth in a detention facility.

This is a reminder that people do not change overnight. Change is a process. Grounding interventions with an understanding of human development theories related to interventions is important to program success for the long term.

THEORY

Simply put, theory predicts and explains behavior. From the natural sciences to the social sciences, theory provides a framework for understanding. Theory influences which questions are asked. Theory directs us where and to whom and when to ask questions. Theory guides empiricism. Best practices and evidence-based practices are guided by theory.

Important for our discussion is the idea that theory guides intervention. Theory suggests what type of programs to establish. It suggests at what age to begin interventions. Theory informs who should be involved—institutions, individuals, or family systems. Theory explains why those interventions are pursued. Theory also explains the results of experimentation and intervention. This chapter presents the theoretical underpinnings of our approaches to urban youth programmatic interventions.

Person-in-Environment Theory

The guiding framework in social work is the person-in-environment (PIE) theoretical perspective. The theory posits that human behavior is best understood as a function of the interaction of the person in their social environment. PIE, as explanatory and predictive, embraces several interrelated theories (Van Wormer and Besthorn 2017). The perspective is reflective of multiple theories that include social, psychological, biological, and spiritual (Dulmus and Sowers 2012). It is an inclusive, holistic theory that incorporates several frameworks for understanding behavior. Those frameworks are often interdisciplinary and can range from the psychological to the organizational (Van Wormer and Besthorn 2017).

The PIE theory allows for the possibility of varying predictions and explanations of behavior. PIE is operationalized across the social work curriculum as a course sequence: Human Behavior in the Social Environment (HBSE). According to Bausman (2012):

> The overall objective of HBSE is to promote a discourse that enhances our ability, as social workers, to make conceptual linkages between multiple explanatory formulations of the person-environment configuration, all while paying specific attention to both social diversity and human development.

The environmental component of PIE involves multiple aspects—international, national, state, city, community, neighborhood, friends, and family. The environment includes not only a physical environment but also a social environment that involves social constructs such as race, ethnicity, gender, and sexuality and values and virtual environments. The person component includes individual and unique psychological, emotional, physical, cognitive, and genetic factors of a given person that interact with the environment. To predict and explain behavior, PIE suggests that we look at all aspects of an individual's environment and also examine individual factors that may contribute to behavior.

For example, we may predict that a person from an affluent family who never had to manage personal finances has a greater risk of financial insolvency than a person from a working-class background who had to contribute to paying rent and utilities for their family during high school. We may explain the reason why a person is reluctant to volunteer is due to a traumatic situation when he volunteered for a classroom exercise that led to embarrassment.

In some cases, environment may be the strongest predictor of human behavior. Environment impacts the languages we speak and our view of the world. It is the exception, not the rule, in which individual decision-making is contrary to environmental factors. We can predict that a 43-year-old banker has a greater likelihood of embezzling funds from a senior citizen's bank account than a 21-year-old food service worker. The 21-year-old food service worker may have a greater likelihood of taking rolls of toilet paper home from the break room than embezzling. Both are examples of individual decisions to steal; however, what they are stealing is influenced by their environments and what they may have access to.

The PIE theory is why we use circles. Creating an *environmental* context for youth to thrive by modeling behavior to shape it in the future is the goal of circles. PIE also influences how circles are utilized as an intervention.

Circles—An Approach to Theory

There is no popularly identified or named circle theory. Utilization of circles is an intervention approach. We clarify that we do not "Columbusify" circles: suggest that a long-existing practice by non-Western people is a new discovery. The circle itself is the result of millennia of indigenous cultural practices that have been time tested as effective. Circles are long effective approaches of human interaction utilized to address conflict, problem-solve, plan, pray, heal, and even celebrate.

Theory influences how the circle is utilized. The type of theory utilized in a treatment modality can be incorporated in the circle approach. As noted, theory indicates what questions to ask and who to involve. The circle can hold a variety of theoretical approaches. Circles can be used in psychoanalysis, eye movement desensitization and reprocessing (EMDR) therapy (Wilson et al. 2018), cognitive processing therapy (CPT) (Wiley 2016; Wilkinson et al. 2017), motivational enhancement therapy (Kells et al. 2019), and a variety of other therapies.

Circles are best viewed as a partner to the PIE framework. Circles are an engagement approach and can be understood as a form of midlevel approach to behavioral change.

Social work theory engages three levels of social work. Micro refers to social work with individuals. Meso refers to work at group levels, and macro refers to greater focus on policy and organizational levels. This is derived from the seminal and ubiquitous work of Brofenbrenner (1979), who expanded the basic three levels of micro, macro, and meso into five levels of practice over his research career (Erikson et al. 2018).

The microsystem refers to the immediate environment (family and friends, those who have direct contact). The mesosytem refers to the connections that the person makes between those in the microsystem between the microsystem and others outside. The exosystem refers to the locus where the person does not have any active connections and is not an active participant (e.g., parent or extended family members' places of employment or other social interactions). The macrosystem refers to the external culture of the person and places this within a regional, national, ethnic, racial, and religious context. The chronosystem refers to how transitions over time have impacts on the person.

Operating from the PIE theoretical perspective, we see circles as an example of meso-social-work functioning at the group level. The goal of the circle is to create an environment that is beneficial so that behavior is positively impacted as a result of a sympathetic response to the environment of the circle. Our argument is that humans succeed emotionally as a sympathetic (positive) response to an environment or in direct reaction to an environment. For example, a youth finds direction, support, protection, challenge, growth, encouragement, and space for leadership in an environment (family/program/team) and moves toward positive achievement of goals. A youth may also find lack of direction and support yet move still toward positive achievement of goals. This is a *reaction* to the environment.

In a commencement address, a person formerly involved in the child welfare as a youth stated: "I am here today because of who you said I was." She was motivated to achieve as a result of the negativity of the environment. She used that as a motivation to achieve. Ideally, however, there is the existence of a supportive environment. To be certain, while the achievement was in reaction to a negative environment, there was required a sympathetic environment outside that family in order to achieve those goals. The circle is one such sympathetic environment.

HIP and Circles

The circle can be a supportive environment. The circle operates in the context of providing a full programmatic environment in which youth can flourish. Flourishing is a condition of subjective well-being. Keyes (2002) notes that the study of subjective well-being is separated into two research streams—the hedonic and the eudaemonic.

The hedonic stream refers to the experience and perceptions of positive feelings and emotions (or lack thereof). The eudaemonic stream refers to overall mental health involving perceptions of potential that when achieved lead to positive functioning (Keyes 2002). Both streams are covered in the seminal book *Flourish* by Seligman (2011), who defines flourishing as a "psychological state characterised by positive emotions, engagement, positive relationships, meaning and accomplishments with various positive work/life outcomes" (Van Zyl and Stander 2014, 265). Flourishing also involves achieving positive life functioning (Witten et al. 2019).

A number of studies (Schotanus-Dijkrstra et al. 2016; Witten et al. 2019) reveal that adolescent flourishing is important, of course, due to its evidence-based connection to mental health, resiliency, academic performance and confidence, social support, and physical health. In a systematic survey of adolescent flourishing literature, Witten et al. (2019) conclude that adolescents who consistently experience negative environmental conditions that may include crime and poverty are likely to engage in high-risk behavior that may lead to the opposite of flourishing: languishing.

These environmental cues lead to cyclic behavior that has a reciprocal impact on well-being. Poor environments that may include abuse contribute to engaging in risky behavior. Risky behavior is frequently reflective of languishing (Venning et al. 2012 and Kwong and Hayes 2017). The review of the literature does indicate that despite these environmental dynamics some youth do flourish in reaction to challenging environments (Witten et al. 2019).

That youth do flourish despite being in environments that are not traditionally conducive to positive adaptation has prompted an area of study known as resilience and persistence.

Woods-Jaeger et al. (2020) identify resilience indicators as including the ability to "persevere, self-regulate and to adapt/improve" (333). The study revealed consistency with "the social-interpersonal model for trauma sequelae, participants consistently highlighted the critical role of social support, interpersonal relationships, and cultural factors in promoting resilience after trauma" (333). The authors importantly note that trauma impacts are mediated by environments.

While there are individual differences in terms of responses to trauma, it is clear that environment is a mediator and moderator of individual responses to trauma. While the environment may produce the trauma, it is also the environment that can lead to positive processing of the impacts of the trauma. The environment (cultural, familial, and programmatic) also may produce the tools to adequately serve as a bulwark against the potential impact of the trauma as well. It may provide not only support but also direction in terms of how to interpret the event or situation and also situate the locus of control. The environment can situate volition.

That is, it can lead to influencing thinking between polarities of attitudes of "things happen" or "we can change things." Environment influences decision-making. The research of Woods-Jaeger et al. (2020) examined resilience in youth who were exposed to community-based violence. Focus group responses pointed to strategies that youth include to promote individual resilience. The groups also revealed how community values not only assist with resilience but also reflect challenges to revealing vulnerability.

A respondent shared: "You're tough and you don't want people to think, like, something got to you, you're sensitive, that you're weak" (Woods-Jaeger et al. 2020). Tilting toward a reason to have spaces such as circles, youth in the study expressed the value of sharing the range of the emotional impact of violent events with others. However, participants noted this value was not reflected in their own social environments (Woods-Jaeger et al. 2020). A focus group response in the study showed that participants would have liked to have a place or supportive individuals to assist with processing emotions, but in the absence of such they kept the emotions to themselves. Youth identified a lack of safe spaces as a barrier to developing community connectedness.

Another study of reaction to violence indicated that community connection is an important emotionally protective factor (Schultz et al. 2016). Community is often framed as a physical place, but here we suggest that community can be framed as a created emotional space. Schultz et al. (2016) argue that community-informed efforts decrease the impact of trauma on individuals.

We describe circles at the center in this book as a direct result of the theories that point in the direction of creating safe physical and emotional spaces and creating a supportive community that decreases impact of trauma and building resilience to lead to flourishing. The research of Woods-Jaeger et al. (2020) revealed that participating youth described experiences of interpersonal and community mental health stigma associated with accessing professional emotional support after community violence exposure. Circles can serve as the programmatic community bridge for youth to access professional support.

It is noteworthy that there has been popular culture acknowledgment of the impact of violence and trauma and the need to seek professional help among youth, suggesting an urban youth environmental shift in the view of gaining professional mental health support. Rapper Meek Mill released a song, "Trauma," that details urban violence. The song was from the 2018 Grammy Award–nominated album *Championship* that debuted at number one on the *Billboard* 200 chart. In 2020 Chicago rap per G Herbo released an album entitled *PTSD* (post-traumatic stress disorder) that debuted in the top ten on *Billboard* 200 chart. In the album, he readily acknowledged, not only on the album but also in media interviews, the emotional impacts of being exposed to violence; he shared that he was diagnosed with PTSD and engages in therapy.

Gaining Participation through Leadership

Many youth are not prone to participate in any programming that involves an outward nod to support of any kind, self-help, or a safe space for expression. The most successful activities are those that involve sports, academic enrichment, entertainment and music, or other activity. Noting this, we strongly suggest that any group attempting to attract youth should have a focus on leadership. The circle and groups around the circle are best framed as leadership groups.

Leadership does not carry any social stigma that may be attached to self-help or programs aiming to assist with trauma, loss, healing, or even gaining life skills. Youth can often be easily recruited with any group that has leadership in the title or a leadership component. It may be a marketing strategy, but this marketing strategy is grounded in the literature of youth leadership. Interestingly, even when participation may be an actual matter of life and death, participation is not guaranteed among youth.

Werner et al. (2019) conducted a study of participation in a congenital heart disease transitional education program for those who were diagnosed with this disease. Participation in the program was not consistent. Positively, however, the study found more participation in younger youth—teens, as well as with those with little knowledge of the disease. This study could not, however, determine whether it was parents, the program itself, or those involved in the program that impacted participation. It is raised here to demonstrate that even in matters of physical health, gaining consistent program participation among youth is difficult.

There is a limitation in the literature related to program participation. Certainly, studies focus on outcomes of participation but not on the motivation to participate. The literature addresses impacts of parent participation but not whether parent participation was the reason that youth participated and to what degree there was participation (Garst et al. 2001; Wang and Fredricks 2014; Walker et al. 2014). Our work suggests that youth participate in *nonmandated* programming when they are affirmed in a setting, they gain immediate rewards and status, they are encouraged by peers and caring adults, and they are self-motivated. Confirming what our work suggests is Bean et al. (2016), who relate that leadership programs should have three components "(a) positive and sustained adult–youth relations, (b) youth life-skill building activities and (c) youth participation and leadership in community activities." Doing so promotes positive psychosocial outcomes.

Many youth, particularly urban youth, are not inclined to participate in programming that has a focus on prevention, safety, education, or life skills unless they are compelled to do so as part of a diversion program linked to avoiding criminal justice system involvement. There is increased resistance based on gender. Young men, we have found, tend to be more reluctant to participate in programs not related to sports.

We operate from the perspective that programs that seek to appeal to young men on a voluntary basis are more likely to be successful when leadership training is a component. There are two reasons: stigma and the continued operation of traditionally male paradigm applied to social interactions. The paradigm is aligned with a youth culture and American cultural obsession with being a "boss." Being a boss is associated with strength, while being in a support group is associated with weakness. In social psychological terms, being in a support group is associated with failure. While decreasing in recent years as there has been a growing focus on mental health and mental health in urban communities, a stigma remains for those who participate in counseling or therapy. Help-seeking activity tends to be associated with weakness and vulnerability. The stigma attached with belonging to a program that is intended to help is decreased as long as it is associated with leadership.

Positive Adult Participation

Bean et al. (2016) noted positive and sustained adult-youth participation. This is a fundamental part of the circle. Youth gain consistent access to positive adults who are the program facilitators participating in the circle. Melles and Ricker (2017) add perspective to the importance of positive adult-youth participation: "Youth participation was most effective when adults took an active role in providing the opportunities, assistance and guidance so that young people could develop their leadership capacity in an atmosphere of trust and respect" (160).

Adults participate; however, youth may facilitate circles as well as provide direction related to session topics. To promote comfort and support, youth are encouraged to speak freely in the circle using words/vernacular that youth utilize. Expletives are allowed as long as the words are not used to demean others. We note that this element may be a challenge for some, but it cements the circle as an environment where youth are affirmed in the presence of adults.

The language of the circle creates and maintains an atmosphere of authenticity. It is also an attempt to create an environment that allows for steady communication without censorship. There is a dual-purpose rationale for allowing youth to speak freely in circles. The first is decrease a hierarchy of authority related to roles (facilitators as rule keepers and adults; participants as subjects and children). The second is to reinforce equity in that youth can communicate in a way that shows them being respected as young adults. It decreases hierarchy and promotes a sense of collective ownership. It manifests in the action that youth, in terms of participation in the circle, are equal members. It communicates safety and promotes the idea that they can be "themselves" related to communication with comfort.

Outcomes

Melles and Ricker (2017) note that review of the literature about youth program outcomes is incomplete. The literature covers specific program outcomes but does not have a comprehensive assessment of which factors influence youth program participation. Combining the theoretical elements discussed above—environment, support, focus on leadership, positive and consistent adult contact, and youth communication affirmation—we contend, lead to increased likelihood of program participation that can lead to positive outcomes. We also note that outcomes often may be realized in the long term.

Human behavior is impacted by knowledge. Youth have to know better in order to do better. Youth cannot outperform their level of awareness. Programming with circles at the center provides an environment that increases awareness. At the same time, experience does reveal that having knowledge does not always lead to better performance outcomes. Knowledge, however, is a necessary component of improving decision-making that leads to decreased risk-taking behavior (Torok et al. 2019; Lipsey et al. 2020).

We stress that change is a process, and that while knowledge is gained, people do not change immediately. Providing knowledge leads to changing thoughts that lead to changing behavior. This change may occur over years. Youth work, however, is focused on youth. That is, outcomes are focused on short-term results. Youth literature is focused on empirical outcomes that are immediately tied to program interventions. An unfortunate gap in youth literature is not having longitudinal analysis of program outcomes. An exception to this is the work of Bilet et al. (2020), who included a 31-year follow-up to cognitive behavioral therapy and panic disorder.

Human development is process based: people may progress, regress, progress, stall, and possibly progress again. We argue that short-term behavioral change is important, but long-term, sustained behavioral change is the goal of youth work.

CHAPTER 3

Program Team Building

Leadership Matters

Lesson from the Circle

A master's degree from an Ivy League institution. Street credibility from years of gang activity. Penitentiary time sharpened desire to give back to communities he said he had taken much from. He was poised in front of largely white corporate and elite audiences who hung on to his words. The audiences gleaned their own sense of credibility by providing a platform for him to speak. Danger lurked from the past, but safety was in the present. They seemed to relish that somehow they were part of his present success while conveniently ignoring that they were caretakers of the structures that were designed to produce at least half of his story.

He was ideal to lead a program that was to change the outcomes of youth who were at risk for criminal justice system involvement. He code-switched with the comfort of a person raised in a town along multiple borders. He had the academic background and the community background to command respect.

However, his authenticity to whom <u>he</u> was grew his credibility with youth and the staff he eventually hired. He connected with parents because he showed he cared about their children. He made home visits, followed up with calls, picked up children, and became a surrogate father at times. He was dependable and responsive. Fifteen years after the program folded, he is still in contact with a number of the youth from that program.

High Impact Practices with Urban Youth—Circles at the Center. Yan Dominic Searcy and Troy Harden, Oxford University Press. © Oxford University Press 2023. DOI: 10.1093/oso/9780197549926.003.0003

LEADERSHIP

The important process of selecting a leader for program development, including the characteristics that youth program managers embody, is the focus of this chapter. Good leadership can inspire, and poor leadership can damage. Leadership is critically important. While books and articles on leadership dominate the business and management literature, they are lacking in the social service and youth work literature.

SETTING A DEFINITION

Exploring leadership across multiple disciplines yields several definitions and conceptualizations of leadership and reveals the complexity of defining leadership as a term (Manolis et al. 2009; Miranda and Goodman 1996). Adding more to the difficulty of defining leadership is that there are even more discussions of descriptions of leadership *traits*, discussions of *styles* of profession-specific leadership, *skills* related to effective leadership, and *paradigms* of leadership (Roberts 2008; Kotterman 2006; Gallagher 2002).

Overall, agreement about leadership tends to center on its complexity rather than a singular definition (Eddy and Vanderlinden 2006). We operationalize leadership as a dynamic process-driven activity that involves role, goals, and influence between a person and a group (Kinsler 2014). The literature also focuses on participant leadership traits or how leadership theoretical models help programs increase effectiveness (DeVera et al. 2016; Iachini et al. 2017).

LEADERSHIP TRAITS

There is a tendency to overlook the leadership traits of the program directors and managers as key components of youth program success. Many focus on the program elements exclusively. A notable exception exists with Tate (2003), who examines servant leadership in youth programs. Tate (2003) argues: "Only as one is truly willing to introspectively evaluate and shape one's approach to leadership is it possible to build a working community in which employees feel valued, appreciated, and heard." Citing prior theorists, Tate (2003) shares: "Effective leadership must consider the needs and values of those being led, and a 'community of shared values' is necessary to generate action around a common cause." Tate maintains that awareness is critical to success. This awareness involves active listening to and being responsive to program participants, coworkers, and supervisors.

In the work of Larson et al. (2016), there is exploration of the leadership trait of balancing authority of position with youth agency. Open-ended learning tasks (those not bound by rules and time frames) and technical learning tasks (those bound by rules and time frames) were differentiated, and hence with open-ended tasks less authority is needed; in contrast, technical learning requires authority and specific direction. The study also revealed what would be expected: It was more important *how* leaders provided direction and advice than that the leaders provided direction.

The ideal approach to providing direction involves being conversational and authoritative, in contrast to being unilateral and authoritarian. Larson et al. (2016) proffered that supporting youth even when they may disagree with decision-making allows for maximizing youth agency. Leadership allows for youth to participate in the conversation about decisions and provides feedback, thus reflecting the value of the youth perspective and acknowledging their contribution. The agency is reflected in the ability to contribute.

Agency is further underscored when leadership allows youth participants to be involved in program planning. Mortenson et al. (2014) cite research indicating that youth often are aware of problems in their communities up to 3 years prior to adults, and that their insights are invaluable to solving problems. Much of the literature on community engagement and youth participatory research focuses on the results of engagement but not on how leadership approaches facilitate this. We recognize this gap in the literature and thus share what we know from our experiences as those traits that are important. Through examples of our work, as well as qualitative data from program participants, we cover the essential leadership traits of effective youth program leaders. Those traits are authenticity, inclusiveness, availability, demonstrating care, and accountability.

AUTHENTICITY

Discussion begins with authenticity because it is the single most important trait for leadership with youth. Authenticity refers to a state of being that is genuine and affirming of all the elements of oneself, both positive and negative. Authenticity also includes an awareness of oneself derived from one's environmental origins, including culture, region, affinities, biases, and motivations.

Many youth tend toward skepticism in relation to adults. They look to character flaws in adults to dismiss their leadership and advice. It is not uncommon for youth to challenge adults to determine whether they are worthy of their emotional and time commitments. In establishing relationships with adults, youth will assess whether their own vulnerability will be valued. They will push boundaries consciously and unconsciously to discover whether their acceptance and treatment in the program is conditional or without condition. Absences without acknowledgment of absence is a common approach that youth will use to determine whether their presence is valued. They want to know that they are missed. Also, youth may challenge staff and leadership with aggressive behavior to determine whether staff will treat them similarly to other adults in their past, who may have dismissed them for behavior. Youth often equate program dismissal with dismissal of them as people. Authenticity moves toward that which will hold youth accountable for behavior yet engage the youth in programming nonetheless and affirming them as individuals.

Program staff are under even greater scrutiny. Being able to relate to someone based on outward traits and characteristics such as being from the same cultural group or neighborhood or even a shared experience is valuable; however, what is the most important is authenticity. This is where participants discern program worth—through the people associated with it, through its leadership. Sharing culture is not enough.

Sharing authenticity and commitment to youth is essential for solidifying youth participation. Pretending to be someone that one is not is one of the surest ways to be rejected by youth. Failing to acknowledge insecurities when called on them by youth is also a sure way to be spurned by youth in programs. Spurned youth do not engage in programming. In basic terms, if youth do not sense that a person is real, then they become the object of ridicule. That ridicule then impacts the program.

It describes authentic leaders as positive, ethical, values driven, and collaborative and notes that in displaying these behaviors, they earn the trust and respect of their followers and influence follower performance. Authentic leadership is considered to be the root construct of positive leadership (Luthans & Avolio, 2003).

Walumbwa et al. (2008) proposed a multidimensional authentic leadership framework comprising four distinct dimensions: self-awareness, relational transparency, balanced processing, and internalized moral/ethical perspective. Assessing potential program leaders on the dimensions is advised in order to reach program outcomes. Self-awareness refers to the personal understanding of strengths, limitations, beliefs, and values. Relational transparency refers to the presentation of one's authentic self to others and how others perceive this presentation and its impact. Balanced processing involves the ability to objectively analyze empirical, qualitative, relational, and opinion-based data in decision-making (Avolio & Wernsing 2008). Last, the internalized moral/ethical perspective is the degree to which the leader is guided by core values and morals in daily practice in contrast to external pressures.

The four dimensions of authentic leadership promote achievement of program goals. Authentic leadership is associated with both individual and organizational outcomes for those working for authentic leaders, including improved mental health and higher job satisfaction (Azanza et al. 2013; Jensen and Luthans 2006; Walumbwa et al. 2008; Gardner et al. 2011; Laschinger and Fida 2014). Authentic leaders set the tone for the program employees as well, create healthy work environments, and promote positive program outcomes (Giordano-Mulligan and Eckardt 2019). Walumbwa et al. (2008) state that an authentic leader's behavior: "Creates and fosters the healthy ethical climate and psychological capacities of employees resulting in greater self-awareness, an intrinsic moral standpoint, relational transparency, and balanced information processing among the followers."

Leader behavior that draws on and promotes positive psychological capacities promotes a positive ethical climate (Walumbwa et al. 2008). Authentic leadership theory emphasizes the importance of ethics and positive role modeling in the leader-follower relationship and proposes that leaders can help their followers achieve positive outcomes. It must be shared, however, that while authentic leadership is a multidimensional construct, research has not fully demonstrated all four distinct dimensions of the construct (Neider and Schriesheim 2011; Walumbwa et al. 2008; Gardner et al. 2011).

INCLUSIVENESS: BRINGING YOUTH AND STAFF INTO DECISION-MAKING

Effective program leadership involves including youth in program decision-making. This reflects program design elements that allow youth to feel ownership, as was discussed in Chapter 1. Inclusion embeds an element in programming to signal to youth that they will be listened to and their voices matter. As a leadership approach, inclusiveness utilizes both formal and informal approaches to incorporating youth in decision-making.

The formal involves structuring program participants into an organizational decision-making structure. This can be done in various ways. One way is organizing a program participant advisory board that meets with the program director for regularly scheduled meetings. The degree of inclusion may range from having the participant advisory board attend the program and/or agency board meetings or have a designated participant board representative regularly present concerns, ideas, and activities to the program director and program and/or agency board. This institutionalizes the contribution of program youth and prioritizes their input and participation. Participants are both formally seen and heard.

Informal approaches to incorporating youth into decision-making are related to accessibility to program staff and leadership. The degree of availability and approachability signals inclusion. A director can skillfully use these interactions as ways to gain input on program direction. Leadership can learn what is happening outside of the program. They find out what is happening on social media and how participants are reacting. Leadership can find out about participant family dynamics and concerns. Leadership can find out what is happening *on the street*. That is, they can gain awareness of activities that involve safety, criminality, and risky behavior surrounding sexuality and violence. This can be gleaned from being approachable.

Having this knowledge allows programming to be responsive to current events and issues. This knowledge may translate to incorporating it into current programming and providing interventions that decrease risk-taking behavior. Additionally, it may provide for interventions that also provide safety for family members and the community at large. It may provide for the free flow of information, which may lead to interventions that address needs for employment, housing support, and educational support, for example.

Youth in low-resource areas may feel as if they are powerless and lack access to those who wield decision-making authority. Being approachable decreases these feelings of powerlessness and increases connection to the program. Feelings of increased inclusion are associated with greater program participation. It makes participants feel a sense of belonging and that they are valued. Inclusion in decision-making promotes positive feelings of powerfulness and agency. The best youth office directors are those with actual open doors so that participants know that the director is approachable, present, and available.

AVAILABILITY

As a leadership trait, this is simply the act of being accessible to program participants and program staff. Ideally, availability also involves being available to participant family members and community members. In smaller programs and in smaller centers, this is, as a general rule, easy and often by design. Space does not allow for distance and inaccessibility. However, with larger programs and centers, it remains advised for a program director to maintain availability. This may be simply making daily walks around the facility and saying hello and learning names to inviting youth to stop by and talk or engaging youth by attending activities. As stated with inclusion, being approachable with an open door is also a reflection of the leadership trait of availability.

Being present is important. Being responsive is important. The nuance between being heard and being listened to is that there is an action component related to being heard. Being heard and listened to should not be misunderstood as taking action that favors the desire of program participants. The action involves responding to the question or to the request. The response may not be an affirmative response. It may actually involve the rejection of a proposal from program participants, but it should minimally involve more than cursory consideration on the part of the director. The action may involve a response that considers data, timing, finances, feasibility safety, or any other contributing factor to the decision. What is important is that action was taken and conveys consideration and thus conveys the value of the program participants' contribution.

Availability as a leadership trait is also beneficial for program staff. Being available facilitates listening, hearing, and action. Thus, leadership should be inclined and oriented to have a professional expectation of accessibility and availability for participants and staff.

DISPLAYING CARE (APPROACHES TO SHOWING CARE)

Much has been written about emotional intelligence in leadership since the concept of emotional intelligence reached the popular lexicon through book on the topic. Our goal is not to revisit a discussion of emotional intelligence but to suggest that emotional intelligence is an essential trait in youth work for interaction with both program participants and program staff. Emotional intelligence is defined as reasoning abilities utilized to discern the emotional state of others and one's own emotional state (Leedy and Smith 2012). Utilized with program participants, of course, it is necessary to be attentive to their verbal and nonverbal communication and also important to be aware of formal resources within the program and within communities to attend to their needs.

It is also important to be aware of informal community resources such as older youth, parents, elders, and religious leaders. It is important to not only be ready with the resources but also demonstrate the care through behavior. That behavior may be to not only share the information with participants but also accompany a participant to access the resource. If a participant may need a referral for a health screening, it is far more effective to have a staff member accompany the youth to an appointment than to simply verbalize that the participant should go. Confidentiality in this example is understood. The accompanying of a participant to an appointment is only if formal permission is granted by parents/guardians. The example is intended to convey that caring is active. Caring is best translated into behavior.

Care needs to be expressed in terms of setting program and behavioral boundaries, expectations, listening, and availability. Youth know that leadership and staff care when they are prioritized with time and accessibility. As shared, youth often challenge adults and program staff to determine the authenticity of their caring. One type of challenge is to assess leadership and staff time commitments. Participants know that staff are being paid. However, participants tend to test staff commitments to determine whether they are present only for financial compensation or present out of a genuine desire to serve youth. Youth are determining whether in the eyes of leadership they are valued for more than a paycheck.

Many of the youth understand the pecuniary value attached to care. Children who are in the child welfare system are intimately aware that their caretakers are receiving money for their care. They are attuned to how they are treated and what caretakers do with the money. They will push and test staff to determine if it is them and their well-being that staff and the director are interested in or if it is money related.

It is certain that as employers it cannot be expected to force directors to work extra hours without compensation. When selecting leadership, it is important that they know that their work hours will not be standard. As a practice, it should be that they will be provided flexibility in their work hours so that they can be available to youth (i.e., for events, special occasions, and emergencies in and outside of the programs). This shows that they care.

ACCOUNTABILITY

Fredericka et al. (2016) provides a comprehensive definition of accountability. They share that accountability has three dimensions. Citing a prior study, they identify one dimension as responsibility: the willingness to accept and fulfill the duties of the position and serve the program, agency, or office. Dimension 2 is openness: the expectation to be linked to one's words and actions. Dimension 3 is answerability: the expectation to explain beliefs, decisions, and actions. Fredericka et al. (2016) succinctly relate that accountability is committing to others, while responsibility involves committing to oneself.

As a leadership trait, it is the commitment to program participants and program staff that is distinctive. As shared, participants will often challenge or test program leadership and staff. Being accountable by manifesting the three dimensions of responsibility, openness, and answerability provides for meeting participant challenges.

To clarify, this does not mean that participants and staff will agree with the decisions; it means that they will come to understand the decision-making process. Confidence in leadership is built knowing that there is openness to providing answers and following up on requests, issues, and concerns. Confidence in leadership is built by understanding where program commitments lie.

CHAPTER 4

Recruitment, Retention, and Participation

Lesson from the Circle
Ex-con. Former street gang member. "At-risk" youth.

These were the labels used to describe . In some ways, they all applied, but in others, fell far short of describing the man.

Father, husband, community activist, developer, and brother are all terms that would also describe him and are far better markers for describing his character. If you did not know him, you would not know that he was also a youth sports advocate and champion of local initiatives involving youth sports.

Although not actively involved in the youth program, some staff had built a relationship with him through general community connections and events. When he heard the youth program was starting a new initiative for young people, he became an informal ambassador, offering suggestions for recruitment.

Using his connection to youth sports, he connected with a local high school football coach who led one of the top teams in the city. Ronald had a specific eye on two of the young men from the football team, an all-city quarterback and a wide receiver. The activist engaged the coach to allow both young men to be a part of the program, knowing that they would also miss important practices to be involved.

The program staff engaged the young men, and they became active participants in all phases of the youth program while maintaining involvement in youth sports. They later went on to college, both graduating and participating in Division I sports, with the quarterback going on to lead his Division I team to victory; the team had not defeated a long-standing rival in 15 years.

Lessons from the Literature

High Impact Practices with Urban Youth—Circles at the Center. Yan Dominic Searcy and Troy Harden,
Oxford University Press. © Oxford University Press 2023. DOI: 10.1093/oso/9780197549926.003.0004

Recruitment of youth for social programs is a combination of both art and science, as when one looks at the various number of programs that exist, from very active to sedentary activities, it is not always clear what the "magic" is that attracts young people across the board. Recreational, athletic, academic, and social programs all have different methods of recruiting. Young people need environments where they can be affirmed, challenged, and supported as they go through the many day-to-day adventures of physical, emotional, and social growth. Although there is literature to suggest how to set up general environments for young people, attracting youth from diverse backgrounds with diverse interests is not without challenges. Different from college or even trade or military choices, high schools, particularly in urban settings, can be segregated geographical enclosures that mirror class and racial differences, privileging the wealthy. Few students "choose" the environment in which they will spend 4 years of their lives and are given choices within this structure to play out their autonomous selves. These choices lean on the ability of school administrators to offer a smorgasbord of options, limited by scarce resources and monitoring. Establishing programs that are both rich in content and engagement and open to diverse youth becomes critical; yet, these programs also "cream" the best students, and young people who are at worst considered "high risk" or, at best, divested and disinterested are left out and struggle to find their way. In this chapter we discuss key aspects of high impact practices (HIPs) for recruitment, including recruitment practices, risk versus asset-based assessment, creating meaning (the cost-benefit equation), and engaging initial participation to retain youth throughout the program.

RECRUITMENT

High impact programs have effective recruitment strategies to engage youth, including effective outreach and marketing. Many programs complain that although they have quality programs, they are unable to either identify or recruit young people, particularly adolescent youth, to attend. A challenge in recruitment is the appropriate matching for young people to the type of program. Is the program targeting a specific type of young person? Has the community, school, or program identified its greatest need or gap in services for a specific type of young person? For example, are quality athletic programs absent in the area? Is this a program that can serve diverse interests or diverse backgrounds? Assumptions concerning youth demographics, interests, and grit can lead to missed opportunities for engagement of young people.

To illustrate, we examine further the lessons from the circle story shared at the beginning of this chapter. Alex was a two-sport star at a selective enrollment high school in Chicago. He was rated as the number one quarterback in the city and was an honor roll student. However, a mentor of Alex knew that he had diverse interests, and although he loved playing football, he wanted to give back to his community and help address the violence that took place, as coming from a single-parent household in a vulnerable community, he had witnessed firsthand many of the more pressing problems in his community. Alex became involved in our program, and through meetings with the coach, he was able to leave practice early at different times to become involved in the program. In addition, the program allowed him to miss certain days to attend football practice. Alex benefited from his involvement in the afterschool program, helped others, and was able to receive a college scholarship, where he went on to become a star and college graduate. The adults and youth professionals, including his coach, were competent, flexible, and supportive in meeting his needs and at the same time provided clarity on what he could and could not do. This allowed Alex to carve his own path, while being firmly supported by adults. Alex proved to be a great match for the program, but others may have overlooked his needs and the benefits for him of being in the program. By being clear on the program goals and making a clear assessment of Alex's external and internal assets and challenges, he was able to be supported by the team.

Matching the youth with the program can include several factors that can help determine the appropriate fit. Below are several questions that can help determine the target group of young people for your program:

Is there a demographic and/or behavioral or attitudinal challenge that they possess that can benefit from our program?
Is there a particular skill, knowledge area, or talent that I believe would benefit them?
Do they have to live, work, or go to a school within a particular location or geographic boundary?

Assessing initial criteria and being clear on parameters can allow for message clarity that providers can use to structure their recruitment efforts. When this is not clear, providers can offer false promises to youth and their caregivers, other providers, and community and lead to disappointment and a poor reputation for the youth practitioner. Assessing a program's capacity early on can provide clarity as well, recognizing the importance of skill, staffing, and environment in creating effectiveness.

Accessibility matters here, as having programs that are easy for young people to attend based on proximity can be important. For example, some providers work with local school programs to access space either during or after school hours. However, this presents a challenge to recruit young people who do not attend the school. Another challenge is safety, as some youth cannot cross neighborhood and gang lines to access programming. Site neutrality, or identifying spaces young people can access, travel to and from safely, and feel welcomed matters. Some programs go as far as to purchase vehicles that can transport young people to and from the site in order to ensure safety and involvement.

Another factor that plays a role in recruitment is competition between programs. Often based on both their capacity and funding, several programs may compete in the same region for young people. For many programs, their ability to attract and sustain funds drives their recruitment practices. Although at this may not be problematic, it can lead to young people feeling as if they do not have the option of choice, as providers convince the young people that their options are limited and they have no other option but to stick with their program. Being able to be clear on programming efforts, the type of youth that the program is able to effectively support and both physical and social boundaries can aid significantly in effective recruitment.

Once these areas are established, youth providers can examine what efforts they need to make to perform outreach to identify young people can take place. As the story mentioned above illustrates, one can engage with the larger community to assist in recruitment efforts. Resources can include

> Schools
> Afterschool programs
> Sports leagues
> Teachers
> School counselors
> School administrators
> Parents
> The local community center or youth clubs (park districts, the Y, YWCA, boys and girls clubs, etc.)
> Court systems
> Religious organizations (churches, mosques, etc.)
> Family physicians and health clinics
> Street outreach workers
> Therapists
> State and city agencies
> Coaches

The list is not exhaustive, however, and providers may be creative in developing a list of any person or place that may cross paths with the young people they are seeking to engage. The important thing to remember is that there may not be one simple place or person that can be the answer to all of your recruitment needs, and that there are many allies that can emerge that can support your work.

After establishing an initial list of potential allies to support outreach, developing a marketing plan can also assist in recruitment. This may include appropriate handouts or flyers that are clear and direct concerning the program, potential benefits, location, and type of young person and public announcements at events, schools, or locations where potential youth and resources are located. One of the most important emerging methods to engage youth, their allies, and providers is the use of social media to connect with the larger community. As well, social media, in its multiple forms, including Twitter, TikTok, Facebook, Instagram, and Snapchat, is an important source of connection. However, demographics associated with age, race, class, and other identity markers reflect usage across different platforms. Understanding the unique platform and usage among the community of youth and their partners can be important for recruitment and marketing.

Having offered the above, it is important to remember that there may be no greater marketing effort than the personal touch, as both youth and community members want to know that the program is safe, is of quality, and has solid people working with it. Involving young people in designing recruitment plans, engaging in outreach, and supporting marketing efforts can add tremendous value to recruitment efforts. After all, "word of mouth" is arguably the most effective method, as youth find each other credible in ascertaining whether a program (or the people working in it) have value. Additional factors in recruitment and retention is the perception toward the young people and whether the program is deficit based or asset based in its approach. To dive further into this, the text explores the importance of determining risk and assets in the initial engagement and assessment process.

RISK VERSUS ASSET-BASED ASSESSMENT

A core component to recruitment is the underlying approach within the first encounter with young people, their families, and communities. Although there is a significant amount of literature concerning the importance of strength-based assessment, the default for many programs and practitioners is to define their relationship to young people based on the problem of young people, fundamentally their "risk" profile. Although well intended, in order to justify to funders and policymakers, providers have to make the case that they are addressing a need or problem area. Embedded within this are beliefs concerning youth reflective of adultism, racism, classism, heterosexism, and ableism where public rhetoric belittles, vilifies, and bemoans youth behavior and attitudes. Adultism can take place when youth providers demonstrate paternalistic attitudes toward youth, as-suming that they always know best for young people simply because of their age (Bertrand et al. 2020). Youth can feel disrespected (Bettencourt 2018) and are excluded from decision-making, including decisions re-garding programmatic, policy, and related practices for youth development (DeJong and Love 2015). The framing of urban youth as poor and of color can pervade attitudes of policymakers and providers, making it difficult not to influence programming based on race and class (Gadsen and Dixon-Román 2017). Heteronormative attitudes can persist as youth providers ignore best practices associated with LGBTQI (lesbian, gay, bisexual, trans-gender, queer/questioning, intersex) youth (Vega et al. 2012). In addition, youth who have physical and mental ability challenges can be stigmatized long before they enter a program and be seen as problems (including being medicalized or doubted concerning their conditions) on entering.

The program, then, is coordinated around addressing "high-risk" youth, and the outreach and marketing, program goals and objectives, and assess-ment tools become points of justification for the program's existence. Let's explore this concept of high risk a bit further.

High-Risk Youth

High risk, often stated as "at risk," refers to young people who have an increased incidences of negative physical, social, or psychological indicators and outcomes. These can include, but are not limited to, poor environment; obesity; substance misuse; pregnancy; sexually transmitted diseases; in-terpersonal and community violence, including intimate partner violence, sexual assault, and gun violence; isolation; peer pressure; bullying (virtual and social media or "live"); depression; anxiety; and suicidal ideations. High-risk young people then, can come from different socioeconomic backgrounds and can be vulnerable to any of these circumstances. In the urban context, although all young people can incur these situations, young people of color, particularly young Black men, are often deemed most at risk, and thus the emphasis on fixing environments in order to serve or exclude them becomes the point of focus. For example, when then-President Barack Obama's administration sponsored the "My Brother's Keeper" (MBK) initiative, which targeted vulnerable boys and young men, particularly young men of color, some critics noted that there had not been a similar initiative to support girls and young women of color (Wogan 2015). One of the programs funded in part by MBK, Chicago's Youth Guidance's Becoming a Man (BAM) program, has received millions in state, city, and private funding for its work to increase positive behavior among young men of color. Its counterpart at Youth Guidance, Working on Womanhood (WOW), has struggled to receive the same amount of funding in turn. When addressing the development of evaluation tools, the researchers encouraged the program staff to focus on pregnancy indicators to assess the program's success. Although they resisted this, eventually they had to adopt the evaluators' wishes in order to adhere to the important standard of what some consider to be a successful, evidence-based program: a randomly controlled trial. Programs are then left to focus on high-stakes performance measures, based on risk level, to determine whether or not they are viable and thus worthy of sustained funding. Although at times important to have, this undermines the overall complexity of factors that can determine an individual's propensity for success or "failure" and limits the understanding of risk to diagnosable and literature-sponsored terms that fail to understand the uniqueness of today's youth as well as the diverse circumstances each young person encounters.

Some researchers note that placing the label of risk onto youth blames the victim of larger structural and institutional forces that place young people in vulnerable positions (Toldson 2019). Some scholars and practitioners suggest that the term "at promise" positions them for better outcomes and places the onus on institutions, programs, and adults to create the conditions for young people to succeed in spite of challenges (Fine 1995). For example, legislators in the state of California agreed to change all language in educational policy from "at risk" to "at promise." From this lens, there is an opportunity to see both the challenges that a young person has and the strengths and assets of this person simultaneously. As many screening and assessment tools are used to justify diagnosis, appropriate placement, and funding, practitioners can at times default to a risk-oriented perception of an individual. To combat this, some researchers have developed tools to address what can be a negative bias toward risk. For example, the Search Institute developed positive youth development asset tools that assess youth resilience and protective factors that highlight which aspects currently exist in young people, as well as what may be absent (Scales et al. 2016). It is our belief that using asset-based tools for assessment can create an accurate picture of the young persons within their environment and build on existing strengths, while addressing challenges that are both internal and external.

RETENTION AND PROGRAM PARTICIPATION

At the point of getting young people engaged, many providers worry about retention, noting that at times it is easy to get youth in the door, but once they start, maintaining their presence throughout the life of the program becomes challenging, particularly in a world that is increasingly changing. The practices illustrated in this text offer guidelines that can lead to successful engagement outcomes; however, providers may ask for specific strategies that can assist in limiting gaps for involvement. Gillard and Witt (2008) offer that youth decide to participate in programs based on the intersection of a number of intrapersonal, interpersonal, and contextual factors that influence their involvement. In their view, youth are "active agents," and factors such as social and peer influence, program content and context, and psychological processes and physical constraints and opportunities can determine ongoing involvement. They offer several "assumptions" based on youth development that guide recommendations for retention, including "(1) youth have power and ability to make conscious decisions about their activities and behaviors; (2) youth experience multiple influences on their program participation; (3) youth desire the opportunity to engage in 'voice and choice'; (4) authentic representation and participation of youth is crucial to all participation and retention efforts" (Gillard and Witt 2008, 177).

The 5 Cs of positive youth development offer a proven example of an effective way of maintaining youth involvement. These include (1) competence, (2) confidence, (3) connection, (4) character, (5) caring/compassion, and (6) contribution. Creating opportunities to develop competence within programs allows young people to gain needed skills and knowledge to be able to thrive in academic and social environments. Assessing strengths can aid in appropriate task development and allow youth to find purpose, building skills to help them adapt in an ever-changing world. Confidence building, done in a safe and supportive environment, can help in testing new challenges and environments, allowing them to see that skill building is a lifelong process, and failures can lead to new learning that builds toward success in the future. By demonstrating caring and compassion, youth workers can model empathy and support, which can help foster youth engaging in caring relationships with others, including their peers.

Formulating positive connections can demonstrate that there are people who will serve as allies in their development, formulating new relationships that at times can provide supportive mentoring toward life goals. Building character can include opportunities to learn about concepts such as integrity, service, and accountability and build on existing strengths, which can aid in lifelong development. Teaching the importance of contributions that they can offer to themselves, their communities, and society can support their understanding that who they are matters and that their evolving can help build a better world.

The 5 Cs can help any youth provider develop a positive framework, utilizing the practices illustrated within this text to engage in youth development. Building in opportunities for youth voice, intentional programming, provision of safety, and engagement in activities where youth can "give back" can be important strategies in bringing the 5 Cs to life (Gillard and Witt 2008). One area to highlight here is the idea of safety in successful retention. Safety can be physical or psychological, as youth can encounter physical threats of violence and also are vulnerable to bullying and emotional and verbal abuse. The presence or absence of security should always be addressed, as at times the mere presence of police can create psychologically unsafe environments. However, there may be times that appropriate security personnel are important to maintain safety at an event. Being able to involve youth in this type of decision-making can create opportunities for youth voice, autonomy, leadership, and character building to cocreate the environments that are best for them to thrive.

Other key factors in retention include incentives and involving family and guardians. Rewarding youth with opportunities to go to events, travel, or receive benefits for program involvement can increase and sustain participation and teach valuable goal setting and management skills. Involving family and guardians and other key relationships can build connections that help maintain connection to the youth, demonstrating that their social and familial supports matter.

The facilities that offer programming matter. During the COVID-19 pandemic, several facilities normally open for youth programming had to close to promote safety. Schools were closed and so was most sports programming. Many reports from young people stated that their parents would often force them out of the house, and there was no place to go. Adults reported seeing dozens of young people "just hanging out" when they should have been in remote learning. In many cases, it was the relationships that youth developed with youth workers that supported them through the crisis, where providers were able to come up with creative methods of engaging young people in safe ways.

In bringing attention to the important area of recruitment and retention, you will find that the approaches offered in this text demonstrate a consistent thread that illustrates the importance of creating an asset-based, caring environment, centered on relationship building that can be both supportive and appropriately challenging for young people. The chapters that follow center on building processes and content that allow the above to thrive.

CHAPTER 5

Discussion Circles

Centering Programming and Crafting Cohesion

Lesson from the Circle

"I'm really not homeless," James began. This was a particularly curious state-ment coming from the resident of the shelter for homeless youth. He continued with earnestness after a brief pause: "I mean, my people don't live that far from here. But when I go home I fall off my square. My parents are smokin' and gamblin' almost all the time. A bunch of people come in and out the house. It ain't cool, ya' feel me? I mean my little brother don't even go to school half the time and he little. When I'm home I'm the one who make sure he go to school and then I'm the one who help him with his homework." Each sentence came with added emotional weight. His eyes stared into mine to ensure that the weight would be carried. Assured, he continued. "But when I go home I just ain't good. I fall off my square. I start smokin' again. I don't do nothin'. So I'd rather be here."

The discussion circle created the setting for James to feel comfortable enough to disclose. He expressed vulnerability, strength, and hope. In a brief exchange, James expressed an unexpected level of maturity in which he chose to sacrifice freedom from supervision for a regimented rule-laden life in the youth homeless shelter where curfews and school attendance are enforced. He acknowledged that he lacked the familial supports to reach his goals and needed the shelter's help. Compassion and regret populated the same sentence. James wanted his brother to excel but regretted that he could not help him while in the shelter. The discussion circle provided emotional security, expectation that his sentiments would be heard, and support.

High Impact Practices with Urban Youth—Circles at the Center. Yan Dominic Searcy and Troy Harden,
Oxford University Press. © Oxford University Press 2023. DOI: 10.1093/oso/9780197549926.003.0005

This chapter focuses on the discussion circle as the center of high impact practice (HIP) programming for at-risk youth. As a best practice, the discussion group serves as the starting point for effective programming. The literature indicates the import and high impact of "peace" circles and discussion circles. The discussion circle creates cohesion and provides a safe space for participation and a reference point for all group activities. The circle sets the tone for the program and is the reference point for participants whether the goals of the program range from increasing frequency of exercise to decreasing criminal justice system involvement.

Our practice separates the elements of the circle into the opening, body, and closing. We have found that while the talking piece is profound, it is not an imperative component for our process. If a participant wishes to speak, he or she is allowed the opportunity. The facilitator is conscious of maintaining respect of the circle within the group.

THE OPENING CHECK-IN

The physical layout of the circle replicates an actual circle. Positioning chairs in a circle or sitting in circles visually represents status equality and connection. It also allows for eye contact for all those who are present, and it allows facilitators a visual connection to all those present. The check-in should take place in a circle when possible. The check-in begins each group.

One goal of the check-in is to decrease the emotional and hierarchical distance between members of the group. Anyone present must check in. There are no observers in circles; all persons in the room or setting should be a part of the circle. The check-in is essentially a welcome ritual to the group and for the group. As an opening, it allows for redirecting focus on the group and preparation for the topic of discussion. The check-in should be not only relatively short but also allow for individuals to share aspects of themselves with the group. The check-in provides an opportunity for participants to gauge similarities and differences among group members.

An example of a check-in is to request participants to state their name and/or what they wish to be called in the group. The facilitator can set a tone by sharing that participants can utilize nicknames or even create a name for the group if desired. The facilitator may ask that after sharing their name, the participant can share who is their favorite musical artist. Music tends to be an easy topic to bring youth together and has the cohort impact of creating a frame of reference for youth. It also allows for intergenerational exchange between others of varying ages in the group.

For example, the facilitator begins with the following: "Please share with us the name that you want us to call you and then share what song that you have been playing the most over the last few days. After you are finished, let us all know by stating, 'I'm in.'" Participants will often verbalize favor or disfavor to the selections, but the facilitator sets the tone for the group by affirming what was heard. The facilitator can repeat a name and the song as an example. Allowance should be given for humor and laughter. A facilitator should not mistake humor for disrespect. Sometimes, there may be laughing and joking during the check-in; however, it is best to model appropriate behavior and gently direct participants to honor what is said by the participant checking in.

The focus should be on maintaining the check-in process. It is more effective if the tone of the circle is punctuated with encouragement versus a tone of control. That is, more attention should be placed on the sharing, not on the enforcement of silence. Attending to control versus cooperation serves to derail the circle and careens the circle into reaffirming status/power divisions in the group.

The check-in provides voice to all members, not just those who are prone to talk. The participants who tend to be quiet and shy have the same opportunity and the same audience to share.

Check-in may be utilized to address a current national or community event. Check-in can also be used to address an issue that is affecting one of the members. An approach to doing this is to raise the topic of the check-in as part of the PIES check in. Participants are asked to respond to the question series: How are you doing physically, intellectually, emotionally, and spiritually (PIES).

For example, for the PIES check-in, some participants may check in under emotional by saying, "I am decent" or "I am fine"; however, participants are encouraged to check in with an actual feeling (happy, peaceful, angry, sad). With this check-in, the facilitator can probe about core emotions related to their emotional state. When a person states that they are "OK," the facilitator may clarify whether or not the person is happy. Additionally, for the person who checks in that they are angry, the facilitator may push the person to disentangle anger from another feeling or to process the source of the anger, such as vulnerability or fear. The net impact is to convey safety within the circle to convey emotions.

Check-ins set the tone for the entire group in three ways. First, they deflate hierarchy of status within the group. Second, they provide a clear opening of the group. Third, they model the operation of the circle. After a participant has checked in, we ask that they state that they are "in." Stating, "I'm in," indicates that the person is present and ready to participate. The collective responds, "Ase," to affirm the person's presence and contribution to the group. It confirms to the participant that others were listening.

Ase (pronounced "ah-shay") is a Yoruba word that indicates affirmation of a statement or can be translated as "and so it shall be." After the check-in, members collectively state, "Ase." This has been used in multi-cultural contexts. The check-in covers all members of the circle. Anyone present is requested to complete the check-in. Facilitators explain that if they do not want to answer the check-in question, they can pass. If a person does not wish to answer the check-in question, then they can pass by stating, "Pass." There is no pressure to comply by *accepting* the request to state, "I'm in." The focus is on presence in the circle, not pressure to verbalize. Presence is viewed as participation.

CRAFTING MEETING GROUND RULES

There are two perspectives related to creating rules for the discussion circle. One is to set the rules for the group in advance. The second is to allow youth to create the rules. Taking the first approach, we strongly suggest having only two rules: no talking when another is speaking, and no mobile phone use while in the group. (We want to reiterate that the group is to be egalitarian. To that end, we allow for the use of profanity. The circle must be a place where youth can communicate in a manner with which they are comfortable. Censoring language equates to censoring experiences.)

The second approach involves allowing youth to create the rules for the group. This is a way to develop buy-in and ownership by youth participants despite the possibility of conflict between the expectation differences between the youth and adult facilitators. It also places the onus of responsibility on the youth to encourage them to enforce their own rules. Facilitators are to stress that the rules should be those that they all agree to abide by. When ownership is gained, participants will police themselves, and facilitators can focus on the topics of discussion. Often, meetings get derailed as a result of too many rules.

PARTICIPANT OWNERSHIP OF TOPIC AGENDAS

A way to secure participation and ownership of the group is to allow for participants to plan what they want to discuss. This is recommended so that students gain understanding that the group reflects their desires and reaffirms that they authentically have status within the group. A facilitator can pass out paper for participants to write down their ideas anonymously. This reduces peer pressures against suggesting topics that may not be popular, and it reduces fears of embarrassment if a participant wants to discuss a sensitive topic.

For anonymous participation, it is good to ask youth to write down the topics they want to discuss and then place the strips of paper in a box. The facilitator should prepare the strips of paper in advance so that they can be folded and placed in a box so no one can see what was written on the paper. The box should be prepared in such a way that no one can peer into the box. The facilitator places the box in the center of the circle and then allows participants to place the strips containing their chosen topics into the box. The facilitator can decide whether to read them immediately or to share them with the group during the following session. We suggest that they be shared during the following session. Some youth may ask who suggested a particular topic and tease other members. It may produce an environment where some may not want to share even in anonymity.

The following session the facilitator should identify all of the suggestions. There may be suggestions that are clearly flippant or sarcastic, but they should be shared. That they were all shared affirms that all levels of participation are considered, and that students feel that their voices are heard and participation matters. It also allows the youth to censor themselves. That is, group members will acknowledge that some of the suggestions were intended to be silly, and they will either rank them low or eliminate them altogether.

The facilitator can utilize a whiteboard or an easel to write down the suggestions. The entire session can be used for establishing the discussion topics for the remainder of the program. The youth are enlisted to rank all the suggestions that have been written. After they are written, there should be voice votes on what topics should be prioritized. Ranking does not have to be in terms of what received the most votes but in terms of what was selected as important to the group. The facilitator can decide what is most important or to operate the discussions around what the facilitator sees as topical and important for a particular week. An important component of this process is that the youth participated and directed their own learning.

This process of ownership embeds participation in the program. In effect, the youth created their own program, which promotes a desire to participate in their own creation. This has the net impact of allowing youth to see that their thoughts and ideas are important, and that adults/program managers hear them. It allows for a degree of self-determination, which translates into ownership of the discussion circle. It also provides youth with opportunities for practicing leadership and developing agency

(Blanchet and Cohen Brunson 2014). Evidence-based practices include the importance of developing leadership skills along with having youth engage in power sharing with adult staff (Blanchet and Cohen Brunson 2014).

Power sharing promotes agency in youth. Power-sharing opportunities for the youth can extend to allow them to facilitate the discussion circles as well. Blanchet and Cohen Brunson (2014) provide evidence of the importance of providing such opportunities to urban youth, particularly Black males. It is indicated that there is a relationship between loss or absence of agency and health and well-being. Program components that include opportunities for agency within the program itself and for opportunities for economic entrepreneurship tied to earning income, which is associated with positive outcomes.

Jennings et al. (2006) posit that power sharing should include not only planning of groups but also opportunities to exercise economic agency. That is, utilizing circles with programs that have opportunities for entrepreneurship that lead to legitimate ways to increase financial viability of the participants is important. Our program findings validate Jennings (2006) assertion that innovation allows for reaching more youth, particularly underprivileged males, and can lead to improved psychosocial functioning.

While there may be a curriculum that is established as part of a program, it is important to have flexibility in discussion circles. That flexibility can allow for youth to engage in more ownership of the process and the group. For example, if there was a community circumstance—a well-known person was hurt or killed, a national news story such as an election, a traumatic happening—then these can all be addressed in the group instead of a topic that was intended to be discussed. This flexibility then helps to allow the youth to witness their ownership of the program.

BLESSINGS AND THE IMPORTANCE OF "HOLDING" A SAFE SPACE FOR EMOTIONAL SHARING

Asking for permission from the youth participants is an important aspect of the discussion circles. This has the purpose of granting youth agency and control and promoting further ownership of the circle and program. Often, youth report not having any input into their daily lives and activities. School, punishments, even foods are sometimes forced on them. Asking for permission is a small programmatic gesture but is often overlooked. Asking for permission affirms that the person has choice. It is an action that builds trust in the facilitators and the process by modeling that youth opinions and desires are valued and honored. Asking for permission also gives the students the power to determine the degree of their sharing and induces greater comfort with the process. It does not put youth "on the spot" to participate.

A key component for solidifying the safety of the space is the opportunity for a "blessing" of participants. The blessing is the process whereby a single participant is surrounded by the circle and positive statements are given. A single participant is asked if they would like to have a blessing. The first time that it is asked, participants will likely have looks of befuddlement. (While it does have religious overtones, it is not a religious activity.) One person will likely volunteer. If not, then a cofacilitator should volunteer in order to model the process. The participants are asked not to share advice. They are asked only to offer positive sentiments about the person in the center of the circle. They are to share an insight or observation that is positive about the person.

For example, if Shawn volunteers to be in the center of the circle, a facilitator can begin by offering: "Shawn, I know that you have the mental toughness to get through this difficult time." Another facilitator or participant models other positive sentiments and adds: "Shawn, every time you come to the program you are smiling and people feel good around you." A final example is: "You have a great way of making people feel welcome, Shawn."

Those among the circle take turns by offering the blessing. Usually, the circle promotes everyone sharing; however, all are not required to do so. When all those who desire to add to the blessing have done so, the facilitator asks if anyone else wants a blessing. The new participant enters the center of the circle, and the process is repeated. It ends when no one else volunteers for the blessing. The blessing is usually saved until the end of the discussion topic. A checkout closes the circle.

For some youth, the blessing is one of the few times that they hear something positive about themselves. It is one of the few times that they hear something affirming from their peers. The blessing reassures them of their value. The activity is an esteem and confidence builder. Because the activity is rooted in the discussion group, the group itself becomes a source for esteem building. The circle becomes a trusted source of support.

AFFIRMING PARTICIPATION

It is important to understand that engagement of participants has a range. There will be those who remain largely silent yet attend regularly. There will be those who are vocal yet have sporadic attendance. There will also be those who are thoroughly engaged. The wisdom of the facilitator is to understand that there will be varying levels of engagement just as there are varying levels of engagement with all human activities.

Success is measured by both the number of youth who continually participate *and* the number of youth who attend sporadically. We keep the groups open even to those who attend intermittently. Some youth may resent others who lack the same level of commitment and may not want their participation. Those youth are to be reassured that the goal of the discussion circle is to create a safe space for those who need it. An added perspective to share is that natural consequences for behavior will manifest themselves for both those who participate consistently and those who inconsistently participate.

Affirming participation, however, should be programmatically built in. The first HIP approach is to reward participation. This has been done through gym time, snacks or meals, financial compensation, outings, grade credits, or ability to participate in a sporting or social activity. A second way to affirm participation is to praise participation anytime a person contributes to the group or anytime someone shares. This is a low-effort yet HIP approach to affirming participation. This also involves acknowledging participation verbally at the end of a session through personalizing the sentiment to the youth. Saying an authentic, "I am glad you were here," affirms participation.

EQUITY IN PARTICIPATION

A key component of the success of groups is to ensure equity in access and opportunity for participation. That is, the group must ensure that everyone can participate to the degree that they feel comfortable. Also to be ensured is that the group holds a particular amount of discomfort but is supportive through the emotional discomfort. Check-ins are an important part of ensuring this; however, they are tone setting, not maintaining and facilitating. Here it is important to scan and assess the room. Facilitators must observe body language and be vigilant that others are not monopolizing discussions.

It is also important to provide the opportunity for a silent person to be included. Comments such as, "I have noticed that you haven't said anything. Is there anything you want to add or share about what you are thinking?" can be posed. Additionally, care must be given not to allow those who are not participating to derail the group by diverting attention to them. This can often be a passive approach to assert power. Knowing that the group will turn the focus on the silent members serves to allow passivity to be a tool to gain attention. To address this, a facilitator can remark: "I notice that you are a bit tense and silent; when you are ready to participate, there is room." This acknowledges their presence and communicates to the person and the group that they see the person's resistance, but it does not detract significantly from the flow of the group.

An approach to increasing equity in participation is to assign tasks to members in the group. One member may have to select the check-in topic and the other the checkout topic. This provides an opportunity (and ownership) for inclusion and does not put a heavy lens of focus on a person who is reticent to participate.

Ensuring equity in participation requires asking everyone in the discussion circle to answer a particular question. Often, this is done when a group lacks engagement, and it is done to generate energy and responsiveness. Other times, it is done so that the same voices do not monopolize the group. Everyone has the opportunity to pass; however, all should be encouraged to respond. That encouragement may involve positive regard, such as: "It's OK; take your time. We heard from others, and we want to make sure that you are heard." Listening is important.

LISTENING AND FEEDBACK

Facilitators must be keen listeners. They also must be keen "praisers." That is, they must encourage those who have participated by offering praise for doing so. They must give positive regard for those who have participated. They must suggest, for example: "That is an interesting point. What do others think of that?" As a HIP, it affirms the person sharing the point and opens an opportunity for others to engage.

Adult participants and program-planning participants as well as the facilitators must be aware that they already have status, power, and an audience for their voice. Attending to this notion will make them a better listener and facilitator. Youth often do not have an audience before adults where their voices are acknowledged and listened to as equals.

Therefore, it is important to make the group the place where youth receive the attention and their voices are heard. They must be prioritized. Too often, adults make the mistake of valuing authority over participation. That is, the focus is placed on the adult displaying knowledge and being a rule enforcer versus creating a safe space for the youth to display their knowledge and have their voices heard. Allowances for the youth to speak freely is important. While it is up to the facilitator, we, for example, allow for the use of profanity. If we are to truly have a safe space and we are to have equity, then the youth should be allowed to communicate in the manner that they are comfortable. Facilitators function best when their professional behavior is youth embracing versus rule enforcing.

Listening is imperative. Facilitators show that they are listening when they are silent. Too often, adults focus on telling youth what they should do or how they should feel. It is more effective to listen and then to provide an example. A guiding aphorism for our discussion groups that is shared with participants is: "Children make mistakes, and adults make choices." The group can provide a venue for the youth to consider options and to have group members share what choices they make. It is clarified that, as facilitators, we will not tell you what you need to do besides making a choice. We aim only to help you think through the consequences of choices.

One such exchange occurred with a young man who was being targeted by a rival gang. He had expressed that he had been shot at and a friend of his was killed by the rivals, and he knew who the shooters were. Essentially, he was telling the circle that he not only was going to defend himself with a gun but also, because he knew where the shooters lived, was likely going to go "get" them before they "got" him. The other youth in the circle related that they understood the circumstances. Withholding judgment, the facilitator stated that he understood, but that the participant still had choices. The young man said that he only saw it as kill or be killed. The facilitator asked if he had family any other places than Chicago. He responded that he had family in northern Chicago suburbs and in another state. The facilitator then asked whether those were options for him and if he could stay with them. The facilitator followed up by discussing the possibility of him staying indoors.

The facilitator also acknowledged understanding that living under the threat of being shot at any moment was extremely stressful and debilitating. It was noted, however, that choice was still involved. Engaging his peers in the circle, the facilitator asked the participants to review possible consequences of him shooting his rivals. The facilitator encouraged the young man to think critically about the net impacts to extended family, friends, and his future if he chose to shoot his rivals.

The facilitator directed the young man to explore his emotions through a visualization exercise to promote his engaging of emotions if he successfully targeted his rivals. The circle assisted by supporting the young man as he examined his feelings of loss of his friend if he successfully targeted his rivals. The circle also examined the criminal justice impacts and the emotions associated with prison. The facilitator concluded the discussion by re-presenting other options outside of the city of Chicago.[1]

We are unsure what choice the young man made. However, we are certain that he was actively engaged in the circle and listened attentively to suggestions. The circle provided a safe place that he could share thoughts and feelings, and it was facilitated by a caring adult in the presence of his peers. He left the circle with more than he entered. He left with support and choices.

CLOSURE

Ensuring proper closure is the final key element of the circle. Closure offers the group an opportunity to transition from the intimacy of the circle to everyday norms. Generally, the circle provides a summary of the major events of the day and encourages all members to participate in sharing the learning that may have taken place. One technique used is to ask what the group's "highs" and "lows" were. This allows participants to give an honest critique of processes and arms circle facilitators with knowledge concerning effective and ineffective elements of the group. It also allows the facilitator to assess the emotional state of circle members before they leave.

Members in a circle often share emotional concerns, such as the young man above, and can be more vulnerable than usual. In the situation above, the young man had not completely resolved his decision, and it was important for him to know that he was supported in preparing to make the best choice for himself. Follow-up suggestions included connecting with trusted adults after the session to ensure that he could continue to process appropriately without feeling as if he was on his own. Good follow-up is essential to HIPs, and ensuring 1:1 connections outside the circle leads to greater transformative possibilities within the circle.

Once an effective summary or next steps have taken place, a checkout can occur. This is an important aspect of the circle as it offers the opportunity for one last "temperature check" within the circle because everyone can share their state of mind that they are leaving with. These can be as simple as one-word checkouts that describe the current emotional state or can be more in depth or even humor-filled. The checkout models closure that many young people do not gain in their lives, as often people come and go without acknowledgment or goodbyes. Participants realize that their voice counts, and that they are important members of the circle and that their presence or absence matters.

CHAPTER 6

Content before Curriculum

Lesson from the Circle

Walking into the facility, one could see the care and compassion that the staff took to make the setting comfortable, energetic, and colorful for the participants. By many accounts, not many people get to see the insides of orphanages. Popular media often depicts these facilities as places where children grow to wait, mostly to age out rather than be placed in the home of foster or adoptive guardians. They are often seen with abusive "guardians," neglectful keepers of warehoused children. The films Annie *and* Despicable Me *are recent examples of films that depicted these facilities as children would rather escape from than live. As this was a country outside of the United States— Mexico, where stories of children "escaping" unaccompanied to cross dangerous territory to arrive at the U.S. border—the expectation that this facility would be no different was there. However, in this place, the energy felt different, if not surprising, to the U.S.-born visitors. However, the visitors couched any enthusiasm for the visit behind practitioner skepticism, as many youth facility administrators play a good front for visitors, hiding anything that may resemble neglect.*

Walking through the hallways, one could see the cleanliness of the facility as the visitors were escorted past neatly kept bedrooms and an arts room. Later, they would see a classroom with children who appeared eager to learn, who greeted us briefly before returning to their studies. Talking with the administrator, one of the guests inquired: "What is the curriculum that you use for the children?" The administrator, fluent in English, but with a notable accent common of native Spanish speakers, replied "a curriculum of moments." Thinking that the administrator did not understand, the visitor asked again: "No, I mean what kind of **curriculum** *do you use for the students learning?" The administrator proudly proclaimed again: "We use a curriculum of moments. . . . We engage learning in both informal and formal ways, realizing that there are teachable moments always around us."*

High Impact Practices with Urban Youth—Circles at the Center. Yan Dominic Searcy and Troy Harden,
Oxford University Press. © Oxford University Press 2023. DOI: 10.1093/oso/9780197549926.003.0006

Youth programs are encouraged to use best practices for designing activities that engage young people. Activities are often derived from standards that are driven by evidence-based research and practices. Practitioners are encouraged to identify these evidence-based practices (EBPs), often in order to procure funding for the activities. Whether it be federal, state, city, or private funders, practitioners are encouraged to adhere to a limited number of models that may or may not be specific to the young people they work with. At best, these models have gone through the gold standard of evaluation research, rigorous, randomly controlled trials with a process that intervenes with a population of youth that the practitioner encounters and a control group who do not receive services. At worst, they are drawn from "Did you hear about this thing they are doing?", interventions that someone in authority recommends for the practitioner to "check out."

Is all content, good content?

Evidence-based practices are generally interventions that have gone through rigorous trials to determine their effectiveness. Initially drawn from clinical trials in medicine, social scientists, in efforts to "prove" the impact of theoretical models, developed a way to assess interventions, generally associated with behavioral change interventions. Several federal agencies, including the National Institute of Mental Health, the Substance Abuse and Mental Health Services Administration (SAMHSA), and the Department of Justice, funded the development of these trials. Those trials that proved effective were then encouraged to be duplicated by those seeking funding throughout the country.

At its best, EBPs help providers wade through many options to engage their participants in positive outcomes and help train providers in effective intervention techniques in order to help those they serve. Critiques include that many of the EBPs that have been developed are designed for populations that the providers do not serve, including in many cases white, suburban, male participants, similar to many research clinical trials. Another critique includes how many urban programs struggle with the research design, citing ethical challenges to offering services for one population (the program group), while denying services to a subset of the same population (the control group) in an effort to "test" the effectiveness of the intervention. Thus, there is a lack of quality EBPs among urban youth of color.

How do I know if an EBP is right for me?

Although there are critiques of EBPs, there are some advantages. Providers, as stated previously, can streamline decisions associated with developing new programs, identify models and curriculum that have already been developed in detail, and receive training related to the implementation. More importantly, funders, in an effort to ensure their funding is being spent in an effective way, can encourage providers to implement models that they believe will be effective, thus ensuring cost-effectiveness and clear outcomes for programs. Consequently, providers can impress on funders that they are adhering to EBPs, or willing to include EBPs as a part of their program, thus eliminating questions related to organizational or program competence. Many funders encourage in their request-for-proposal applications several options for EBPs, including referring to lists developed by the larger federal funding institutions mentioned previously.

Below are a few questions providers and policymakers can ask when considering whether or not to include an EBP or to develop one on their own with the assistance of program evaluators or researchers:

1. Do I have a proven intervention for the program I am developing?
2. Has the proven intervention gone through a randomized controlled trial?
3. Has the intervention been tested for a population similar to the one I serve?
4. If not, is it a similar population?
5. Is the curriculum or program accessible for a cost or free?
6. Does training for implementation and follow-up come with access to the EBP?
7. If I choose to develop my own program model, am I interested and/or willing to partner with a researcher/evaluator to "test" this model?
8. Am I OK with participants being randomly selected, meaning from a pool of potential program participants, with one group being selected to receive the intervention and an equal number not being selected who will not receive services at the point of intervention?

The questions above are not exhaustive, and other questions may emerge. The point is that any selection of previously developed programs should be well thought out and inclusive of staff and stakeholders who can form consensus about the integration of this tested model. Having assessed the questions above, the following material now takes a look at what may be most important concerning development of your own quality program.

THE "HOW" VERSUS THE "WHAT"

Many program models emphasize the content of curriculum, and providers often spend a significant amount of time combing through new and innovative ideas for programming. The emphasis is often on "what youth need" in terms of knowledge or skills, but few take the time to understand critical aspects of "how services are delivered" and miss out on key aspects that include recruitment, engagement, and referral.

As the story at the beginning of this chapter illustrated, the managers of the orphanage were more interested in how their staff interacted with the youth, rather than what the youth were being taught. The content mattered, but not at the expense of understanding and developing methods to effectively engage the youth in participating in programming and extracting the necessary learning that could take place. Here, *process* mattered more than content. By process, we mean the philosophy, methods, and practices involved in engaging young people in important activities deemed to assist the youth in achieving key objectives and outcomes.

ASSUMPTIONS CONCERNING YOUTH OUTCOMES

For example, the Search Institute's 40 development assets are clear indicators of what young people need to enhance or develop intrinsic resilience and extrinsic protective factors to achieve positive outcomes. Implied is how to create this, but not necessarily explicitly in what this process looks like. Little is often asked: "What makes a successful youth practitioner?" Youth practitioners, often front-line workers with little training, are hired with the assumption that because they are young, formerly "at-risk" youth themselves; possessor of degrees in the social services; how they look (assumptions concerning a certain race, gender, class, ability level, language, or sexual orientation); or simply just because they are "willing" to help. In many cases, skill level does not go beyond "what worked for me," individualized experiences that may or may not connect with the youth in question. As everybody who wants to be a parent does not necessarily make an effective parent, recognizing what tangible and intangible skills, knowledge, and values workers possess can mean the difference between a quality program at best and an abusive, toxic, and unsafe environment for youth at worst.

Almost annually, the media reports stories of abusive youth facilities that take advantage of a willing funding stream but deem themselves unsuitable for youth development. Many providers engage in illegal acts, which range from warehousing youth to actual physical and sexual abuse in the name of providing a so-called quality program. However, the literature is filled with examples of safe and positive programs that engage young people effectively and provide quality outcomes. Often, though, new providers are left with guesswork in terms of effectiveness, often because of the nature of high turnover in the field and the "success" of stellar administrators and practitioners. The most talented often don't stay in one position for long, and programs are left scrambling to sustain quality practitioners.

So what makes a quality youth practitioner? Here is a list, followed by examples of what this can look like in action. The YIP former youth worker and executive director offers these six traits for an effective youth practitioner:

1. Rapport
2. Sincerity
3. Balance
4. Humility
5. Objectivity
6. Attitude

Rapport: They possess the ability to engage a wide variety of youth, and young people enjoy their company. They know when to engage with humor and also can relate to young people without relinquishing their maturity.

Sincerity: They "mean what they say" and "say what they mean." Understanding that youth have keen radar, they know that young people respond to adults who they believe genuinely care for them. In addition, they are authentic and demonstrate their sincerity with actions congruent with what they say.

Balance: Their lives are intact, and they are not "messy" with their relationship with the youth. Their life issues don't play out with young people.

Humility: They have a willingness to learn and grow, recognizing that they do not always have the answers, and are eager to seek professional and personal growth opportunities.

Objectivity: They understand their own biases and do not project them onto youth, recognizing the individuality that young people possess.

Attitude: They see the potential in each young person, recognizing their unique gifts, but also recognizing flaws and behavior challenges as often defenses that cover young people's deepest needs (Meunier 2020).

In the example at the beginning of the chapter, although there were obvious instructional practices, educational standards, and the like, the administrators of the facility were clear that education for the youth went beyond the classroom or the group and included every aspect of the living experience for these young people. "Moments" became meaningful, and the staff embodied this as no opportunity became too big or small to engage the young people, even if the "teaching" was subtle and not over the top. In making choices on curriculum, practitioners can consider the following elements:

What is the atmosphere I want the facility and staff to project? Will this be consistent across staff, including intake, assessment, food, group facilitation, and so on?

What are long-term and short-term outcomes that I want for my participants? Am I looking for behavioral, attitudinal, or other changes that allow me to measure this?

Do my overall activities match my outcomes? Do I see a clear pathway for success?

Are there special values, credentials, skills or talents that I want staff to have? Is there a specific training or set of trainings that all staff should attend?

What Is the Atmosphere I Want to Convey?

The atmosphere in a program includes the physical space of a setting and how staff and young people interact with it and each other. Other terms used to describe atmosphere include "vibe," "energy," or "ambiance." Settings can be aesthetically pleasing and culturally relevant to the group, such as having colorful paint on the walls and art, including photos and paintings reflective of the backgrounds of the youth; or they can be neutral in appearance but have welcoming and comfortable furniture that allow people to feel relaxed. Staff may be serious and solemn or fun loving and joking, but they convey a sense of belongingness to the program that helps young people feel comfortable. There is great flexibility concerning how one sees this developing, but the point is to also know the things you do not want to see. When one provider we know was in the beginning stages of his program, he recalled the time he was at a youth program and the youth were ordered to say silent and keep their hands to themselves as they walked hallways, walking in pairs with hands crossed over their chests. The provider felt that children should be full of energy and life, talkative, if not orderly. She wanted to ensure that her new program would represent the latter. Recognizing this, she considered staff and curriculum choices that would bring this to life. Her desire to create this came out of her values for youth programming.

Outcomes and Impact: What Are the Outcomes I Want to See Happen?

Although the language of outcomes and impact has become standard in program practices, including everything from standards of grant writing and program evaluation, the necessity to be clear about this moves beyond pure function. Outcomes shape a program and considering impact allows the provider to think about short- and long-range effects of the program on the young person and their communities. In simpler terms, outcomes tend to be measurable objectives over a specific time period, while impact refers to the broader and longer range implications of an intervention. For example, a program may seek to increase healthy eating habits of young people as an outcome of its intervention. A broader impact may be to increase visibility of healthier lifestyles in their communities. Harder to measure, and subjective in nature, it nevertheless can be part of the vision that a practitioner has in created their program for a select group of young people. By giving thought to this, the provider can consider the who, what, when, where, and how of their program, considering the people, set of interventions, location, and delivery that best align with their intended outcomes. Curriculum choices can then align with the outcomes desired. A provider can ask: "Is there an evidence-based model that exists that has generated similar outcomes for a population like mine?" or "Do the set of practice interventions I have in mind help our young people to get to the outcomes desired?"

Values, Skills, and Talents of Staff

An aspect of ensuring that people are prepared is asking whether or not there is any particular training or skill set staff need to become facilitators or do the work. Although staff are often hired with backgrounds in youth development, a provider should never assume that the training was adequate or done the way that they imagine. Aligning needed training with staff skill set can mean the difference between maintaining and sustaining staff and spending resources inefficiently.

Aligning the program values with the values of staff becomes important here. Creating the space early on to assess what's important to all persons involved can reduce future headaches. For example, in some of the circle practices referenced previously and further in this book, the first things that we established among staff was what values they brought to the program and what values they wanted to create with each other. This clarification allows the team to understand their own motivation to work with youth and to assess how they may be similar to or different from others. There is generally no right or wrong here, but hearing from each other early allows for a cocreation of collective values that can center how providers work with each other, the young people, and the external environment. It can also help with clarity concerning curriculum choices. For example, one youth program found it important to promote youth independence and interdependence through wilderness retreats that gave the young people experiences in nature, learning self-sufficiency through camping. However, the team was decidedly operating on the principles of nonviolence, and an external provider who was seen as an expert in the field was also a gun-rights advocate who felt strongly about incorporating the safety and importance of firearms. As this did not align with the core values of the program, the providers were able to make a decision that would best fit with their program's purpose.

The provider may also want to ensure certain skills of the youth practitioners and assess whether or not they already had the skill set or knowledge or whether they were adaptable to training. At times, programs rush through this process, giving little time to orient staff on both their program philosophy and do not allow enough time for adequate training. Taking the time on the front end to establish a training timeline and protocol can be beneficial to ensuring long-term success and development of staff. In one program that held restorative practices as a core philosophy, the team thought it adequate the youth workers understood basic elements of the principles, and because they had demonstrated that they were excellent youth workers, would easily be able to pick it up and execute programming with the youth. This proved to be problematic, as although they were smart and eager to serve, in part due to previous work experiences, they were unable to shift toward a new model of practicing. It was decided by the team that they would go through more extensive training. As a result, they came back from the training with a new insight and vigor and were able to successfully implement the model to outstanding results.

Once having established the type of person and team one wants to develop, now curriculum is introduced.

CURRICULUM AT LAST

The provider may already have an idea on the type of curriculum they have in mind or may be at a point of seeking new models or creating one from scratch. Either way, by establishing the atmosphere of their program, the outcomes and impact they want to see happen, and the type of people to be on board, they can align their intervention accordingly. We found that whether it is evidence based or informed or built from scratch, the important thing is to ensure that it demonstrates the ideals we mention above, as if the intervention is not culturally relevant; conveying the philosophy, attitudes, and wishes of the leadership and staff; and difficult to implement, it will not be effective in getting needed results. The curriculum, then, becomes the manifestation of the core values of the team and demonstrates a way to bring the program to life in the lives of participants and reflective of a model that all involved can take pride in delivering and sharing with the young people involved. The "moments" then become meaningful in that they are touchstones toward a greater long-standing impact on the lives of the youth.

CHAPTER 7

Fostering Youth Leadership

Lesson from the Circle
They already were successful—at least by standard measures. They were high
school graduates. They were current college students. But many were not
thriving. Faculty members approached with concern about a number of their
Black and Latino male students who appeared unengaged. A sentiment was
expressed that their lack of academic achievement was not due to lack of ability
but due to lack of interest. This was not unique to this particular university; it
was a national dynamic that spawned Black Male Initiative programs to in-
crease retention and graduation rates of males.

A meeting was called inviting campus Black and Latino males. To increase
attendance, food was provided. Convened by faculty and administrators, the
first meeting attracted about 40 students of the 10,000 student population. The
meeting was explained as a desire to bring together the young men to increase
their academic success and to provide support and encouragement. Also explained
was that the conveners, other Black and Latino male university employees, were
only to be the facilitators, not the leaders. The group, if desired, would be about
the student participants and what they wanted. The meeting times, the fre-
quency, the subject matter, all would be determined by the youth.

It was agreed that a group would be formed when the question was placed
to the meeting participants. Did they even want a group? That took almost no
time for agreement. Then it was asked what the name for the group would be.
A brainstorming session began, facilitated by a faculty member. A standard
easel and paper and whiteboard setup yielded several names. A process of elim-
ination of possibilities began. The participation sounded equal parts auction
and political campaign debate. Then emerged the name of the group: BroSE,
the Brotherhood of Scholarship and Excellence. Then the same process led to
the mission statement of the group. Eight years later, BroSE continues. BroSE
members themselves established study groups and study times and community
outreach to area grade schools.

High Impact Practices with Urban Youth—Circles at the Center. Yan Dominic Searcy and Troy Harden,
Oxford University Press. © Oxford University Press 2023. DOI: 10.1093/oso/9780197549926.003.0007

This chapter is not intended to provide a theoretical background on youth leadership. It is not an attempt to visit the leadership literature about youth. It is about practical ways to foster youth leadership. In Chapter 2, leadership was discussed in the theoretical arena. Here, we move to the applied discussion of leadership in order to gain and maintain participation in youth programs. Talking about problems, the need for help and support, and the need to be linked to resources, tends to be associated with weakness and vulnerability. Leadership, being a leader, is not associated with vulnerability, so as such it is likely to gain more participation. As shared in Chapter 2, programs focusing on problems, stressing the need for help and support and the need to be linked to resources, tend to be associated negatively with weakness and vulnerability. Programs focusing on leadership and providing leadership opportunities in contrast is viewed positively as strong in an urban context and as such is likely to gain more participation.

CREATING OPPORTUNITIES FOR LEADERSHIP

It is important to utilize programs as opportunities for youth to contribute and by doing so increase their likelihood of continued participation in programming that will lead to positive substantive behavioral changes. Embedding youth contributions in a program consistently is a high impact practice. A program in its best version provides for the intersection of positive adult interaction, youth autonomy, volition, discovery, and actualization. Providing short-term and long-term evidence of all of these elements to the youth participants themselves leads to high levels of engagement. Youth participants need to see that they are contributing and see the results of their contribution. Providing consistent programmatic opportunities for contribution for youth to lead is imperative and will cement continued participation.

As a best practice, we can learn from organic examples of youth organizations known as gangs. Youth move to the organizations because there are opportunities to contribute, there are opportunities to be rewarded for those contributions, their voices are heard, communities of peers and adults recognize their contributions, and they gain status as a result. Ideally, youth programs mirror these dynamics, but positively.

There are four ways to foster youth leadership: formally, contributionally, representationally, and informally. Formal leadership refers to appointment to advisory boards and/or appointment to fixed leadership positions.

Contribution leadership involves but is not limited to project management roles, project participation, planning participation, and recruitment. Representational leadership involves youth being allowed to helm their own advisory boards or similar groups with limited adult input. Informal leadership refers to recognition as associated with or a member of the program group. Initiatives that focus on leadership skill building are related to positive program outcomes.

The key component of all of these ways to encourage youth leadership is participation. By virtue of active participation, youth engage and are more likely to reengage. They are able to see that their contribution has impact. Contribution and activity can build self-esteem. Activity and achievement establish a platform from which self-esteem can spring. Youth are likely to return to those activities that build self-esteem. They are likely to further engage in activities, which can fuel good feelings about themselves. They are likely to engage in those activities in which praise and support are attached. Including opportunities with attention to providing praise, direction, and support is quite important to increase participation.

The praise and support must be substantive and not merely based on showing up to a program. Every participant is not to receive the proverbial trophy. In terms of the work that the youth are doing there must be critical praise that is based on performance. Lack of achievement is also to be noted. Lack of effort is to be noted. Important is that direction and support for improvement is to be provided. That is, participation can be praised, but it is not to be a substitute for achievement.

Youth who do not achieve stated goals or meet established expectations for behavior should also be addressed and directed toward expectations. Achievement will be rewarded. Participation gains attention, but it is not a sufficient condition for consistent positive regard. To be clear, attending a program is indeed positive and can be complimented. However, it is not a sufficient condition to receive praise for achieving outcomes.

FORMAL LEADERSHIP

Formal leadership is leadership that is recognized by peers themselves, staff, and boards. This is leadership that is built into the operations of the program. The youth may be voted in or appointed. The dynamic here is that it is part of the programming. These elements should be included in program planning to embed leadership as a high impact practice.

A youth advisory board may take multiple forms. It may be established without a hierarchy but is a collection of participants who are a subset of all program participants who operate in an advisory and consultative manner to program leadership and a board of directors. They should actively be included and not merely symbolic. It is suggested that they meet regularly—monthly—and meet at least quarterly with the agency or program board of directors. This provides certainty to program participants that their voices are heard directly by program leadership.

Another type of formal leadership is a youth board of directors. The board is to serve as the body to raise programming ideas as well as voice concerns about program direction. This board can serve as training and professional development for program participants. It may also be useful to form a youth executive board (e-board) that is a standing body composed of traditional leadership positions, including president/chair, vice-president/vice-chair, and secretary. Here, this e-board is to be youth self-directed with minimal adult program staff direct involvement. Adult staff can and should provide support and direction but should not sit in on the meetings. It is to provide an opportunity for youth control and autonomy. The role of the e-board is to make program recommendations. The chair or president of this board represents the youth on the program or agency board of directors. This board should meet quarterly as a standard board would meet.

Separate from the e-board, an opportunity for formal leadership is to create a staff liaison position. The staff liaison is a participant who is identified as the participant representative to the staff and leadership. The participant staff liaison should meet regularly with the program director. Ideally, this participant will be part of the youth e-board and operate distinctly in a role separate from the e-board president. The youth is not in an executive position but a communications position. It is meant to formalize the participation of those program participants who may not wish to serve in a higher profile and responsibility position on the e-board, which tends to advantage extroverted individuals.

We caution to make certain that all roles given to youth are substantive and not perfunctory. If there are too many youth leadership roles, it may not be a positive experience for all since it may dilute the ability for youth to make significant contributions and provide feedback where they can see their contributions. Youth are savvy enough to know the difference between actual and performative program influence.

CONTRIBUTIONAL LEADERSHIP

Contributional leadership refers to opportunities for youth to participate in project planning and project management, recruitment, and project participation. Important components here are that youth are allowed to lead and their voices are not only heard but also incorporated. Often, while youth may be part of planning, their voices are overpowered by program staff. With contributional leadership, a program facilitator must be aware enough to both direct and relent when youth are suggesting ideas. There is value in allowing an idea to be pursued despite a program manager knowing that it is likely not to be successful. Part of the process of discovery is experimentation and exploration.

Participants should be allowed to fail. Lessons exist in the failure. Many program staff do not want a failed project, but this is, perhaps, a greater teachable moment than redirecting or forbidding youth from pursuing a particular project. Participants can benefit in two ways. First, they can see that the adults/program staff supported them despite resistance and thus build trust in the program. Second, they are able to witness the results of their own volition. They can see the lack of success of the project and own their role in it. However, program staff must be wise enough to know what type of project to allow for youth to fail (a presentation to funders may not be the wisest choice). The staff must weigh the possible negative outcomes of allowing a problematic idea to be pursued (of course, safety and legality concerns should be primary).

A key consideration here is providing programmatic space for youth contributions and placing their ideas into practice. It is important to attend to providing space not only for sharing ideas but also for action and execution of the ideas. Contributional leadership taps into the idea of power and empowerment. Youth are often in positions as subjects versus agency. Contributional leadership provides agency.

Too frequently, legal status as a minor is often equal to marginal status. Youth are constantly reminded of their class status of having few recognized rights. Their behavior is often a reflection of aiming to exert power as they have a tacit understanding of their powerlessness in a society. Providing avenues for contribution enacts agency and provides power.

Staff leadership and program directors must be aware and allow for this contribution. It must be embedded in the program. Youth contributions should be discussed openly with board members and program staff. If it is known and transparent, then it minimizes the controversy if any arises from a less-than-stellar project. It is important for program staff to know that youth contributions are a part of the programming and linked to long-term program outcomes.

Related to project management, youth should be designated to assist with managing the project once direction has been established. While their ideas may have been shared, it is important to embed agency in the process of executing the project. This could be a place to formalize a youth participant as a project manager, or it can be a place to identify the entire planning group as responsible for particular aspects of the project. (Examples abound from youth theater projects, which include set design, to costume design, to ticket sales and promotion.) Project managing is an ongoing process that allows for consistent contribution, steady feedback (from adults/peers/community), steady opportunities to see evidence of contribution, built-in accountability, skill development, and discipline (establishing tasks and timelines for task completion, utilizing technical tools such as software to assist with project management, and improving communication skills with peers and adults).

Recruitment is an element that tends to be ignored in program planning. Youth often attract other youth. Incorporating youth as recruiters is ideal. Often, programs will utilize young program managers for recruiting; however, we have found that when youth themselves are the recruiters for participation it has greater and more robust results. A formal program utilizing youth to be recruiters is recommended. As the program itself is being planned, a formal recruitment plan utilizing youth should be included. Programs often have recruitment plans but they do not have youth figuring prominently in the plan. Youth attract youth.

When attempting to attract particular youth, it is important to have a youth recruiter other youth identify with or aspire to become. Identifying with includes but is not limited to having been raised in the same area, having experience with similar circumstances, having similar affinities, and having similar academic achievement. This does not mean only to attract one type of student. It means that recruiting can be done by multiple youth with multiple affinities in order to diversify overall participation. The suggestion is to include youth in order to facilitate recruitment. By having youth facilitators it will increase responsiveness, decrease reticence (being approached by adult program staff or school officials, e.g., teachers and counselors) to participating in a program. It again embeds youth agency and increases the likelihood of recruiters participating and buying into the program. It increases youth investment and links to a greater likelihood that they want to see the results of the program that they helped recruit for. It also solidifies leadership opportunities early in the program process, which will lead to program participation.

REPRESENTATIONAL LEADERSHIP

Representational leadership refers to providing participants opportunities to lead themselves with limited adult supervision. Representational leadership differs from contributional leadership in a distinctive way: it may be considered participation, but it is not intentionally about a project that has been orchestrated by adults or is part of the overall project or project plan. That is, representational leadership is about youth controlling their own space (self-determination) within the context of the program but without any demands from the program. While youth may utilize the space for program planning, it is deliberately unstructured. It is deliberately intended to be an autonomous youth-directed space.

This may be a bit of a misnomer as it is referred to as representational but its purpose lies in that it represents the youth themselves, not the youth as representing or speaking for youth related to the programming as in formal or contributional leadership. Preferably, there is no established hierarchy to this group. While formal leadership established youth leadership for the program and outside of the program, this group space does not need to replicate it. The youth themselves can identify how they choose to operate. It is simply a space. It conveys ownership within the framework of the program. It is an opportunity for youth to represent themselves to themselves. There is no reporting out necessary unless the youth decide this. It also represents the youth themselves to other youth.

A related element of representational leadership is the need for youth to gain self-esteem through their association with the program. Often one of the first desires expressed by youth in programs is to have T-shirts or SWAG (stuff we all get—merchandise that is free that conveys exclusivity related to program participation or attendance). This is aligned with representational leadership. Youth want recognition for their association. They are "representing" the program and themselves and status derives from it. The status is a positive reinforcement to program participation. They must see themselves and also see themselves being seen by others.

Attending to maintaining space for youth independent of adult direction may be a practice easy to ignore or omit. However, we offer a caution. This space has a significant impact on maintaining youth participation. Participants have active agency in a nonhierarchical manner. This arena rarely exists for youth.

INFORMAL LEADERSHIP

Informal leadership refers to elements of program participation outside of planned activity. This is leadership linked to representation by virtue of being associated with peer participants and community members. Those outside of the program may view participants as leaders because of their association with the program. In some ways, informal leadership can be viewed as an organic byproduct of embedding formal, contributional, and representational leadership into program planning. Informal leadership is strengthened by the positive visibility of the program.

Those who are associated with the program receive positive feedback and are viewed as leaders independent of their formal roles in the program but by virtue of them being part of the program. In effect, because they are involved while others are not, it communicates leadership. The participant has made a choice to participate, and this choice manifests a leadership quality.

A RECOMMENDATION

We paint a picture that youth leadership should be tied to all elements of a program. Active engagement increases the likelihood of participation. Embedding youth leadership aims to increase initial participation and maintain participation along with increasing the likelihood for postprogram interaction and follow-up. This is not simply an exercise in planning or representation on boards, for example. Youth can be included in the minutiae of convening meetings, facilitating meetings, leading check-ins, and closing meetings so that they have an active visual, substantive presence.

We stress that contributional, formal, and representational leadership are enacted with program staff supervision. As noted, with informal leadership it is important to provide youth with spaces where they see themselves and see their contributions. It is also important to not only have the opportunities for leadership but to positively reinforce through shared positive public and personal regard about those contributions.

We note again to recognize that extroverted personalities may be more inclined to participate in all of the four leadership contexts. Program staff need to recognize this inclination and allow for the less gregarious to participate while recognizing the privileged status of the extroverted.

Strategies such as rotating facilitators or randomly selecting facilitators can be utilized to do this, as can utilizing group facilitation techniques that allow the voices that are not automatically voiced to have an opportunity to speak and share. For example: "Micah you have been quiet all session, and I know you are a deep thinker. Is there anything you want to share?" Also opportunities for participants to leave notes or to text or direct message input utilizing social media technology as a means of preserving anonymity can be creatively utilized so that all voices can be heard and participation is not limited to the extroverts who may be advantaged through the program leadership structures. Ensuring leadership opportunities for all youth cements a positive program experience.

CHAPTER 8

Retreats

Lesson from the Circle

The COVID 19 pandemic soared into March 2020 like an eagle and stayed around like a crow in a fast food parking lot. For the next 12 months the pandemic impacted every aspect of life around the world. Particularly hard hit were education and urban community-based programming. No longer were youth able to be engaged with afterschool programs, drop-ins, and direct in-person programming due to the threat of the COVID-19 virus. Attempts were made to provide support through online activities, but there were limitations and no effective substitute for direct human contact.

A former program participant of a Black and Latino college male retention and graduation program who was now the director of a similar program reached out for some assistance in planning a retreat. He wanted to produce an online retreat. He shared that his retreat participation was among the most impacting experiences of his college life.

Memorable about his experience was that the person who drove him to the retreat had only planned the ride as a favor but decided to stay after being invited in for a snack. As the snack time ended, he was invited to join a circle that was soon convening. With certain reluctance, he joined the circle. (Of note is that the male neither identified as Black or Latino.)

The topic of the circle involved sharing related to family experiences and the impact of those experiences on their masculinity. The recently invited guest's reticence receded, and he began to share. A casual invitation led to a heroic vulnerability. He was wounded, and while he shared, tears uneasily rested at the corners of his eyes, then seemingly knowing that they would have a cushioned fall decided to slide down more readily. Self-consciousness receded to emotional freedom in the circle. He stayed the remainder of the evening.

No doubt recalling that event and his own participation, PJ shared that he wanted to do a retreat for his program because the retreat was so impactful.

High Impact Practices with Urban Youth—Circles at the Center. Yan Dominic Searcy and Troy Harden,
Oxford University Press. © Oxford University Press 2023. DOI: 10.1093/oso/9780197549926.003.0008

> But he cautioned: "I want it to be a bit light; I don't think we should have retreat-level crying." I teasingly replied that I think he coined a new term to describe a deep emotional response as a "retreat cry." I agreed to assist with planning. The online retreat focused on goal setting and preparation for another semester during the pandemic. While planning, a facilitator shared: "I think we should call this a 'charge' not a retreat. We are going forward!"

The impact of retreats can be felt for decades (Jacobson 2021). They range in form and intent. They can be leadership focused (Gartner-Manzon and Gilles 2018) or related to spiritual; religious (Tori 1999); cultural (Fiddler 2008); political (Taranova 2010); strategic planning (Guanci and Medeiros 2018); wellness (Treleaven 2019); and professional concerns.

The retreat concept is a millennial human practice (Knox 2016). It has its roots in cultural traditions that suggest that departing from daily practices allows for clarity, reawakening, new perspective, meditation, rest, self-reflection, and community reflection. Elements of retreats are manifested in rites of passage traditions, spiritual monastic traditions that can be traced to early Egypt (Knox 2016). Nearly every cultural tradition has some type of retreat. Stepping back or stepping away is a valued human tradition. It continues to be practiced because of its impact. It has potential impact on the individual who participates and on the community where the individual returns. For the individual, it can be an awakening, clarifying, strengthening, or simply restful. For communities, retreats have impact as those who return often return with new or enhanced contributions.

There are two goals of this chapter. The first is to stress the importance of planning retreats as part of youth programming. We do not aim to replicate the myriad guidebooks available online and in print for content of retreats. The specific elements to address in the retreat will be determined by program directors and the goals aimed to achieve. The second goal of the chapter is to present 10 elements to include when retreat planning.

- Establish goals of the retreat: why do it?
- Where should the retreat be held?
- When should the retreat be held?
- How long should the retreat be?
- What elements should be included in the retreat (physical fitness, breaks, fun, alone time, walks, food, snacks, youth responsibilities, ground rules; lights out and lights on)?

- What about facilitation selections and leadership?
- Who should be in attendance (staff, students, board members)?
- Who is part of the planning?

WHY THE RETREAT? GOAL SETTING

Being intentional about the retreat is critical. Retreats may be part of a tradition; however, without adequate direction, effectiveness may be limited. Without a known goal, a retreat is simply a program event without an anticipated outcome.

Planning should establish the goals to be achieved, and those goals ideally should be outcome based. Those goals should be measurable and aligned with the overall program goals. For example, the youth retreat may be focused on improving academic outcomes, such as high school or general equivalency diploma (GED) completion. An overall program goal may be to increase academic achievement. The retreat, then, should focus on exercises that promote this outcome of diploma completion. A program may have this component as part of a crime deterrence component, but it should be focused then on academic completion, and evaluation should be constructed to measure the effectiveness of the retreat at promoting diploma completion.

Outcome-focused retreats can affix empiricism to preretreat and postretreat activities. For example, a survey can be conducted that questions whether school attendance, grade point averages, academic preparation, and/or enrollment in academic programs increase. Empiricism tied to programming is likely to lead to short-term goal achievement for a retreat and greater overall program outcomes.

It has been found that one of the best ways to signal retreat goals is to craft a theme. That theme can be crafted by program staff in order to set the goals; however, as suggested in Chapter 3, collaboration should occur with the youth to increase their level of ownership and likelihood of participation. The theme should be a public sharing of the goals of the retreat. A theme can be embedded in the title of the retreat. It can be either direct or indirect.

Utilizing the example of improving academic outcomes, the title of such a focused retreat should reflect academic outcomes. For example, a retreat title "Preparing for Success One Step at a Time" shares that a retreat is focused on preparing for achievement. A title of "Getting that Paper to Make that Paper" signals the link between diploma completion and financial security. With the theme, seek collaborative input from the youth.

Once the goal is established, then activities of the retreat should be crafted to achieve those goals. There can be secondary and tertiary goals as well, but those goals should be in direct support of achieving the primary goal. For example, a secondary goal is to increase understanding of how current behavior may not be consistent with articulated goals; it is clear that raising this awareness with an activity would likely increase the awareness necessary for changing behavior to make academic progress. Exercises that increase self-awareness and the connection between behavior and outcomes would be encouraged. Also subgoals or tertiary goals such as increasing program participation or deepening the involvement of youth should be aligned with overall program goals. The idea here is not to simply engage in retreat planning to have retreats as a program component. It is to have retreats as a method to improve program and youth outcomes.

Finally, measures to ensure safety should be adhered to, including consent to attend from parents or guardians; background checks of staff, facilitators, or mentors who attend; appropriate transportation measures; and clear safety guidelines for participants and staff while in attendance.

CHOOSING A LOCATION: WHERE SHOULD THE RETREAT BE HELD?

The wisdom of millennia should not be dismissed when selecting a retreat location. The location should be away from the standard location of programmed activities. Removal from physically familiar spaces often leads to physical and emotional discomfort, which create a fertile soil for seeding for behavioral transformation (spiritual, emotional, professional, intellectual). To further use a gardening metaphor, before seeds are planted, the soil is tilled. It is disrupting the settled in order to create room for new growth. Physical removal from standard activities promotes individual reflection.

Part of the tradition of "going away to college" is based on the premise of removing from the familiar to grow independently. Monasteries and priesthoods have historically been in remote locations for this reason, along with removing from distractions.

Ideally, planning for a retreat should be included in budget planning for the program. Costs related to space rental, transportation, and staff support for the retreat should be included in budgeting. If a budget allows, it is recommended to find locations a minimum of an hour away from where a program is located. One reason is to allow for the physical transportation process to impact transformation—carrying from the familiar to the unfamiliar. It is also recommended that the retreat location for urban youth be rural.

Camp-based retreats fulfill this purpose. Camps provide familiarity related to bedding and electricity access, yet Nature provides a backdrop for immersion into the unfamiliar to produce a different experience and awaken discomfort that encourages reflection on a new experience.

In instances where transportation and travel is unavailable, a suggestion is to change the environment of the retreat if it is in a standard programming space. That is, decorate it differently, hold it in a different room, or rearrange furniture. The retreat is intended to be a different physical experience.

Sleeping arrangements should be made that allow for monitoring of participants without being intrusive. The spaces can be specifically dedicated retreat sites or sites that simply have space for participants. It is important to include access to showering/bathing/toileting facilities; sleeping based on gender; kitchen access; and easy access to outdoor activities. Often, retreats are synonymous with camping and a return to nature. This is not required. There can be consideration for selecting retreat sites that reflect a more contemporary or even luxurious mien. Such settings can be aspirational for youth. Hosting a retreat at a hotel or a college campus are examples of aspirational locations.

WHEN SHOULD THE RETREAT BE HELD?

Far from obvious is planning for when the retreat should be held. Ideally, the retreat should be held at the juncture between when relationships have been forged (where participants are familiar to the staff and trust has been built and gained) and when progress toward program goals need attention. For example, if a program is a yearlong, then the retreat should be planned for three-quarters of the way through the program. If it is an academic year, then it should be planned around spring break of the academic year. This is not for practical reasons; it is reflective of the timing of relationships and trust and the timing related to goal achievement.

For youth to participate effectively, they need to have developed the relationships that allow them to feel sufficiently comfortable to take a risks. Also, it is important that relationships have been built between the program and parents/guardians to allow for youth to accompany the program on an overnight retreat.

At the same time, there needs to be something from which participants are retreating "from" (environment that may not be facilitating reaching goals or a lack of personal focus) and retreating "to" (gaining a deeper understanding of oneself as they embark on completing goals or setting goals). This is usually three-quarters of the way through a program's completion. If it is a multiyear program, then it is recommended that a retreat occur at yearly intervals. If it is a multiyear program and new participants are consistently cycled in, then it is important to be mindful to include those who have participated in the retreats in the planning. We suggest, however, not to retreat for the sake of retreating but to reiterate that it is from the standpoint of linking the retreat to attaining program outcomes. Arguably, the process of retreat and the impact that it has on participants will positively impact outcomes (both short term and long term).

HOW LONG SHOULD THE RETREAT BE?

For many youth programs, the retreat is dictated by the available time within the program as well as the available time on a school calendar. Weeklong retreats may be prohibitive. Weekend retreats are what we recommend for two reasons. The first reason is that the time frame is not intimidating for participants or their families. They may be willing to leave familiar surroundings for 2 days but not for 5. It is also a possibility that there may be a financial implication for the family if a member is not present. For example, the participant may be working to contribute to household income. Also, the participant may have child care or elder care responsibilities, and time away would cause too much disruption for the family. Second, the intensity of the retreat is best condensed into 24 hours, and it is difficult to sustain intensity over 1 week. For youth whom this may be their first time away from home/family members, it is better to limit that time away to limit anxiety. The intensity that is amplified by the unfamiliar can be decreased by limiting the number of days away. Additionally, if a participant is attending for the first time, it is advised that a short time is best for an introduction to retreats.

Just as personal trainers tend to gradually build the intensity of workouts, our approach is to gradually build the intensity of retreats. We take that approach related to the programming of the retreat as well. We suggest a weekend retreat that begins on a Friday night and ends on a Sunday morning. It is a 2-day retreat spread over 3 days. Friday during the day is for travel to the destination. Sunday afternoon is for return travel. The first session on the Friday night is meant to engage, share expectations, and build capacity. The retreat full day builds intensity, culminating in a Saturday night "crescendo" session. Sunday is a building, preparation, and lessons learned session. In some ways, this can be viewed as a play in three parts. For youth, it is better to have short and impactful sessions owing to attention span concerns.

We suggest that the sessions should be no longer than 2 hours. According to an adage: "The mind can only take what the behind can allow." That is, if a person becomes tired of sitting in one place, figuratively and literally, then their ability to process and attend to the information being shared becomes diminished. We also recommend that after each session breaks are a minimum of 1 hour to allow for individual reflection and processing. It also allows for an emotional break to decompress from what may have been highly emotional circumstances of shared vulnerability or intellectual challenges. We expect the Friday session to be 2 hours. Saturday programming will be roughly 14 hours. A Sunday session will be 3 hours.

ELEMENTS TO INCLUDE IN THE RETREAT

The retreat should build on these elements: physical, emotional, and inspirational/spiritual/intellectual/aspirational/behavioral. Sessions and breakouts should be structured around a minimum of one of the elements. We often begin the Saturday session with an early morning wake-up that has a 30- to 45-minute physical fitness activity. This has the dual purpose of making this a gender-sensitive experience where male-identified youth can be actively engaged in an activity that tends to privilege their experience while later activities tend to privilege female-identified youth. It also provides a framework for understanding that the human experience involves mind, body, and spirit. All parts of the human experience are covered in the retreat. The morning exercise is also meant to actively awaken all participants and prepare them for the day. The morning exercise will be on Saturday and Sunday mornings. It indicates that the retreat will be active.

During all parts of the retreat, we suggest including snacks and food. For youth (and adults, too), this is an important component. It indicates support and comfort. We have found no need to put rules around snacking and snack time. Certainly, there are designated times for breakfast, lunch, and dinner; however, snacks are available during all parts of the retreat. We suggest having an all-access snack/drink table that participants can utilize without restriction. Whether it is comfort or it is recognition of youth appetite, snacks and snacking will provide a needed support and boost to activities. (Choose snacks from the range of healthy to traditional cookies and chips, soda, water, and juice.)

We also recommend having the breaks planned between sessions of at least 1 hour. It can be used to decompress and to process the information from the prior sessions but also can be used to take a nap, take a walk, or snack.

The ground rules of the retreat should be shared at the outset of the Friday evening session. These ground rules should be agreed on in the circle. Discussion about the rules should be in the circle, and agreement about the rules should be in the circle as well. As with all youth activities, the youth voices should be heard and their recommendations included. The expectation for behavior should be clarified and include discussions about expectations related to substance usage, sexuality, timeliness, and overall participation. The schedule should be clarified, and the youth should be made aware of the timing of wake-up calls and when the call for lights out will be. We recommend that participants are not policed related to lights out. If students want to remain awake, they can, but they must be mindful of others. If there is a designated sleeping area, then that area can be monitored to keep it quiet. However, if the meeting area or a lounge area is possible, then participants can stay there without any staff direction. It is just important to share that there will be a wake-up call at the designated hour and that they are aware of the expectation for exercises about 30 minutes after wake-up call. Allow for 30 minutes before the wake-up call and the first exercise of the day.

Pacing of the retreat is important. After the fitness session and breakfast, the first session of the day should involve reflection and an activity. The second session of the day, after lunch, should be a focus on emotional health and intellectual exercise. The third session of the day should be about emotion and inspiration and reflection. The Sunday session after fitness should be about behavior and addressing behavior and should be inspiring to maintain that behavior after the retreat.

> Session I: Tone-setting reflection
> Session II: Emotion and confronting a challenge
> Session III: Moving to confront and share emotion/spirit
> Session IV: Active engagement: intellectual/inspiring
> Session V: Aspirations and behavior change

In all of these sessions, the circle is to be utilized. However, there should be actions or activities that invite participants to reflect on their own (e.g., to write). There are elements to include to gain deeper engagement. The sessions above are theme related, but it is up to the organizers to plan for specifics.

FACILITATORS

The sessions should be facilitated by staff, yet provide encouragement for participants to engage via breakout sessions and/or steady opportunities for all to engage. These retreat engagements may involve anonymous participation in exercises, such as dropping questions or ideas/feelings in a hat or bag; posting reactions on an easel prop board; or writing down ideas in a journal. Because of the emotional weight of the sessions, it is best to have the professional staff direct and facilitate, which removes self-consciousness and possible criticism from the youth facilitator from the participants.

The planning for the themes of the retreat may came from participants but not the actual facilitation of sessions. Additionally, it is recommended that monitoring of fellow participants only be conducted by staff or nonprogram volunteers. It is important to maintain that the retreat is participant focused—all participants, not just leadership. It is important to establish a nonhierarchical approach to the retreat. The focus is on all participants.

ATTENDANCE

All able to attend should attend the retreat. It should not be utilized as a reward for attendance as it is part of the regular program planning and is a component. All those who participate gain from being present, so attending the retreat should not be an explicit incentive or reward. Regular program staff should attend. To staff the retreat, it is suggested to have one program staff member for every five to seven youth participants. If there are not enough program staff, then volunteers should be enlisted who are familiar to the program. Those volunteers can include teachers/board members/mentors. We do not suggest parents or guardians as this will likely decrease the level of participant sharing involved. The familiarity that participants have with the program staff will contribute to an environment that allows for more vulnerability to be expressed.

While planning may have set the sessions, there is time to make adjustments to the schedule and to the content of the sessions based on what was revealed or addressed/expressed in other sessions. Staff who are not directly facilitating can be tasked with scanning/observing the retreat in order to make recommendations. The staff allow for supervision and safety as well as being able to monitor the retreat proceedings.

Planning for the retreat should be initiated and coordinated by the program director. The program director and the operations team have the ability to identify elements that need to be addressed during the retreat. There may be interpersonal dynamics that require attention during the retreat. For example, there may be social media bullying issues that require attention. There also may be groups or cliques that have formed in the program, and sessions can be tailored to increase interactions between groups. Additionally, a trauma related to the loss of a program member (staff or participant) or family members due to violence may need addressing; community issues may need addressing.

Additionally, there may need to be attention placed on transitions or motivation or visioning for the future. These themes that are directly tied to the weekly program are best assessed by program staff. While there are several retreat session ideas that can be gleaned from guidebooks, it is important that they are not randomly assigned but are tied to program issues and tied to desired participant outcomes. For example, conducting a ropes challenge course or a trust fall is arguably only relevant if there is a tie to issues that participants need to overcome. If self-confidence and facing fears is important, then a challenge course may be a way to address it and prompt discussion about fears, behaviors, and achievement.

It can also be used to discuss changing perspectives about how to change. Neurophysiologists are now indicating that it is actual behavior that is the best way to change behavior (Huberman 2020). This challenges the idea that changing thoughts is the most effective way to change human behavior. Changing behavior by engaging in the ideal behavior is viewed as an effective way to change thoughts and mood and feelings.

Including a ropes course or trust fall just because it is fun is not a sufficient reason for inclusion. This is not to state that recreation is not important. Indeed, as stated before, breaks and snacks are important. Recreation should be included in the planning but as part of a whole-person experience that combines the physical, emotional, spiritual, and intellectual components. Programming should address all four, and retreat planners should select those elements that directly address all four.

Retreat planning is the only part of program planning that should not include participants in the specific elements of planning. They can participate in the broad themes or contribute to the elements that they believe should be addressed, but because they are actually participating in the retreat themselves as an immersive experience, they should not be aware of the specific elements of the retreat. To clarify, participants can know the length of the retreat and the theme of the retreat and can contribute to crafting themes and what issues could be addressed, but they should not be aware of the actual retreat session elements.

The participants need to experience the retreat in a similar fashion as the other program participants. Part of the retreat is to decrease the hierarchy of participants. It is meant to establish equity within the experience of the retreat and not to privilege more active planners. Privileging may decrease the active participation of other participants during the retreat. The retreat aims to renew, not to replicate patterns of participation.

CHAPTER 9

Crafting Celebrity and Celebrations

The Importance of Public Events for Presenting,

Performing, and Uplifting Accomplishment

Lesson from the Circle

The title of the program was Full Circle. The program brought together youth from two differing neighborhood areas that cut across cultural groups and gang affiliations. The program intended to decrease violence and gang activity. Key elements of the program promoted critical thought and community-based participatory research. Among the components of engagement was video logging, producing public service announcements, and providing social media analysis. At the conclusion of the program, a graduation/recognition ceremony was held.

Downtown Chicago in a skyscraper, home to a major university, was the setting of the graduation ceremony. Wafting into the room that held a small stage was the smell of catered food that was soon to be served. White linen-covered circular tables adorned with settings and event programs were arranged banquet style.

The friends and family members of the participants were invited to witness them receive awards. This was the final event of the program. The audience also included officials from the program's granting bodies.

Emceed by the program director, the evening shared with the audience the mission of the program, the activities of the program, and the achievements. A documentary produced by the participants was shared. Materials produced by the participants were distributed (three magazines organized around themes from their community-based research), and speeches were made.

Smiles emerged from the participants and could not be restrained. No feigned coolness or aloof reserve was evidenced among the participants.

High Impact Practices with Urban Youth—Circles at the Center. Yan Dominic Searcy and Troy Harden,
Oxford University Press. © Oxford University Press 2023. DOI: 10.1093/oso/9780197549926.003.0009

> Genuine pride was abundant, perhaps because those who were present completed the program. It started with over 40, but this ceremony counted around 10 participants. Not all participants had family and friends in attendance, however; yet, each participant beamed.
>
> The celebration reflected their agency—they planned the program from food selection to the order of the program.
>
> This was a celebration not of forced participation, not of an institutional rite of passage such as high school graduation, but this was a celebration of self-selected activity. "I used to think that all men were bitches," casually commented one of the participants in one of the vlogs. "I mean the men I saw in the neighborhood were never about nothing. Y'all showed me otherwise."

ACHIEVEMENT

Celebrations are human institutions and social constructs. These constructs have existed since the time of recorded human history. Evident in all cultures, celebrations as institutions convey norms, values, and expectations of behavior. Social programming for youth has focused more on the overall rites of passage process but has not given enough attention to the importance of celebrations and celebrity for youth and youth programming. There are developmental reasons to support and to build celebrity and celebrations into programming.

To be clear, we operationalize celebrity as that which propels participants into public recognition of their program participation and achievement. It is associated with publicizing participation. It is associated with linking celebrity to positive self-esteem (Searcy 2007). It is associated with building a positive-feedback loop into participation. Recognition leads to increased likelihood of continuing participation. Celebration is operationalized here as building recognition and providing accolades to program participants at formal intervals or at program conclusion.

Previously, we covered motivation and addressed intrinsic versus extrinsic motivation. We are only revisiting this discussion here in order to frame the importance of celebration to youth programming.

Law et al. (2012) summarize much of the extant literature related to motivation and human behavior. Citing an earlier study that promotes the importance of environmental influences on behavior, Law et al. note that learning "depends on the experience and feedback from the environment."

Law et al. (2012) also cite classic behaviorist Skinner (1953), who proffered that "positive consequences and feedback for a behavior increase the likelihood of its recurrence, thereby reinforcing the relationship between behavior and the various environmental stimuli present at the time the behavior occurred." Recognizing positive youth activity and participation consistently will also provide greater likelihood of program participation and solidify positive regard between participants and staff.

The authors categorize the reinforcements as stimulating and affective. Stimulating reinforcement rewards include the positive presence from peers, significant others, and community, while affective rewards include the receipt of praise, sympathy, and respect from significant others. The authors add humanism to their assessment of human behavior and motivation by sharing that humans are motivated by a tendency to enhance their functioning.

Interestingly, the authors suggest less reliance on external rewards in contrast to verbal rewards. We challenge that assertion. We do not believe that there is a need to choose. We suggest that it is important to do both. We are most interested in outcomes and not the ontological argument of what motivates behavior leading to outcomes. We are interested in motivating and changing behavior. Theories need not be unnecessarily exclusive. We do not need to choose between internal and external rewards. We consistently stress that adolescents respond to environments. They succeed or fail in reaction to those the environments. Law et al. (2012) offer: "A significant person recognizing the good deeds of a child or adolescent with warm and supportive verbal and nonverbal gestures can initiate the individual's internal organismic enhancement.

Interestingly, academic articles spend little time on the importance of recognition of youth participation and celebration of youth achievement. There is a focus on goal achievement, educational achievement, but little literature on the importance of recognizing achievement and embedding it within programming. Articles focus on motivation and program outcomes, but little is done to address the importance of celebrations. There is much attention in the business and corporate literature on employee recognition and an entire industry built out around employee recognition but surprisingly little in the literature in relation to youth recognition (Craig 2017). We note that the same benefits that make employee recognition important are the same benefits to recognizing youth: increased productivity, retention, building positive program (workplace) environment, increased motivation, increased collaboration, and improved program outcomes (profits) (terryberry.com 2021). Our discussion is separated into those categories.

INCREASED PRODUCTIVITY

Traditionally in the corporate workplace, increasing productivity is viewed as leading toward increasing volume related to items manufactured or billable hours. This also includes service maximization within contracted hours. In youth work, we operationalize increased productivity as increasing participation and attendance in programming. In the corporate workplace, there are many approaches to increasing productivity.

Those range from decreasing waste, efficient staffing practices, and expanding the size of the workforce. In youth work, there are also many approaches to increasing productivity attendance, ranging from incentives to participation (open gym, gift cards, food, trips, and even direct payments). One that does not gain as much attention is what we focus on in this chapter: publicly recognizing youth.

Youth recognition—publicly acknowledging and celebrating program participation on a regular basis contributes to improving program attendance. The recognition can take several forms. While awarding trophies or certificates can be the common ways to recognize participation, an overlooked approach to recognition is to provide T-shirts.

In nearly all programs, T-shirts carry a certain amount of currency and credibility. T-shirts connote membership, status, and style and provide visual recognition of belonging. Among the first requests that youth bring to activities is a desire to have T-shirts or jackets. This is a tacit understanding that T-shirts provide recognition and deliver status to the wearer. This type of recognition should be managed by program staff. Many programs involve youth in logo design and may provide awards for the successful entry. This has a twofold return for recognition—celebrating the designer by the award and celebrating membership and participation by the wearers.

T-shirts are just one approach, but other wearable items include wristbands, necklaces, hats, and even socks. Visual representation of membership conveys pride to the wearer and outward recognition of membership to the greater community/institution.

RETENTION

Note that in this chapter's Lesson from the Circle there was a high attrition rate. We turn to sports to gain an understanding of attrition and to provide programmatic background on how this can apply to youth programming. Citing earlier research about achievement motivation, Gardner et al.

(2018) found that beliefs about ability and achievement goals are associated with enjoyment and the desire to continue in youth sports. Those who believed that their abilities can be developed versus being natural experienced more enjoyment and desire to continue in sport. Those who did not believe that their abilities could be altered experienced less enjoyment and less desire to continue in sport. They were, of course, more likely to drop out. This suggests a need to focus on providing opportunities that demonstrate achievement early on in programming rather than later. It also suggests a need to build in opportunities to demonstrate achievement and recognize it.

This has the purpose of motivating for more attainment and further participation. Additionally, it provides insight into why some youth may simply drop out. If they believe that the locus of control for them is outside of their abilities they are less likely to engage. If there are no results and no recognition or the results are delayed, then they are less likely to engage to the degree that they will realize the benefit and be motivated by self-directed goal setting. They will not be engaged enough to move from extrinsic reinforcement to intrinsic reinforcement and engagement. Gardner et al. (2018) share that it is the lack of enjoyment that leads to attrition.

This also indicates a need to engage more youth in planning (a leadership component) so that programs reflect elements that participants will enjoy. There is need to recognize balance, that is, the fun with the fight or the chill with the challenge. Simply put, if there is no balance, participants will "grow or go." But, we are clear in understanding that it is not simple to show youth that their participation is part of their growing. Celebrations and celebrity are ways to acknowledge this.

BUILDS POSITIVE PROGRAM ENVIRONMENT

Recognition builds engagement (Craig 2017). This also leads to a positive program environment. When participants know that they will be recognized or realize that behavior can be recognized, it can lead to more engagement with the program and also build a positive environment (White 2015). This environment contributes to participants following the model of program staff to recognize other participants and staff for their contributions. That this occurs leads to maintaining a positive program environment. That is an environment in which participation is regular, rules are followed, and staff and participants are respected for their contributions.

The program environment impacts not only program participants but also staff. It creates a positive-feedback and support loop that allow students who may not be traditionally "seen" made visible for contributions. They also may be part of communities where they are objects or subjects to be studied, helped, pitied, or controlled to become those who are agents. As agents, youth become the creators of solutions as well as advocates to activate change to systems that marginalize their status.

Too often in many communities, those that are seen are those who are negative and contribute to the destruction of community rather than those who contribute to the building and sustaining of community. A common aspect of urban youth interactions is practice of playfully demeaning one another, more commonly known today as "roasting" but has historically been referred to as "playing the dozens." As a result of roasting, youth are more exposed to negative comments rather than positive comments and recognition. Recognition orients youth toward positive affirmation and creating an environment or space where they are positively celebrated. There may be youth who have few experiences of positive regard. This regard may not come from family members, school officials, peer group, or social media; however, if the positive regard comes from program staff, it is likely to contribute to greater participation. It may be the place that they turn to regularly since positive affirmation and recognition are in short supply elsewhere. The positive environment is reinforcing and leads to motivation to continue in programming.

INCREASES MOTIVATION

The motivation in employees is related to the motivation to continue to contribute as well as the motivation to work at a high level of excellence. In youth work, the motivation is interpreted as a drive to continue to attend and participate in planning. This also includes contributions to the program as well.

The recognition elements should be embedded within the planning of the program to take place at key intervals. Some programs may choose to do so at the end of each program meeting, or it may be a monthly item. The importance, however, is that the recognition must be authentic (White 2015). The recognition must be substantive, meaning that it must recognize an achievement. Attendance can be an achievement, but we would suggest that it is tied to a contribution independent of merely showing up. Certainly, attendance can be a component, but it is argued that the recognition should be for attendance *and* contribution. Questions to ask related to decisions to recognize contributions may include the following: Did the participant complete a training? Did the participant contribute to a project? Did they meet with program staff? What did they do?

We are suggesting that program staff engage in recognizing verbally, being attentive to program contributions, and then formally making it known that there have been outstanding contributions. This should be done regularly and formally. Formally indicates that it is a regular part of programming, and it is not incidental. It can be done during a snack time or meal time. It could be done as an aspect of planning at the end of each month. It can be done as a certificate presentation or a social media post. It can also be done as a part of the convening or closing of a circle.

The recognition, however, must have these elements—be public (others, including staff, participants, community) are informed of the contributions; be authentic (the behavior identified is substantive and is shown to have improved behavior, a process, or a condition); and be regular (embedded in programming at expected intervals). Doing so has the impact of increasing the likelihood of the recipients to participate. It also increases the likelihood that others will be motivated to contribute in order to gain recognition.

INCREASES COLLABORATION

In much of the discussion about recognition, we have consistently discussed contribution. A primary lesson from the circle is to provide opportunities for youth contribution. We are clear to demarcate between competition and contribution. We do use a corporate model as an example to emphasize the importance of recognition; however, it is important not to create an environment of competition.

To that end, we argue that it is important to view recognition as a way to identify contribution and not to only recognize the "best" or to create a numerical or symbolic ranking system. Competition suggests that those who are not top performers can be marginalized or eliminated. Programs, of course, are intended to provide opportunities for the marginalized and to increase their likelihood of participation. Status can be gained from the recognition, and we do not want to replicate or duplicate social status dynamics outside of the program that cede only recognition to dominant performers. It is not about ranking someone's performance; it is about recognizing performance. To that end, we argue that it is important to view recognition as a way to identify contribution.

By recognizing contributions, it increases likelihood of collaborating with other program participants as well as collaborating with staff and engaging the community. The collaboration may be responsiveness to taking on additional roles, volunteering for leadership opportunities, and/or increasing attendance. It also may lead to more trust building and turning to program staff to assist. They begin to ask for help when there is less fear of judgment and they are viewed as a partner.

IMPROVES PROGRAM OUTCOMES

In a corporate environment, improving program outcomes is related to increasing profits and profitability. Of course, here in youth programming, improving program outcomes is related to assessing whether the program outcomes met the establishing learning objectives or the established learning goals. If the program learning objective is to decrease at-risk behavior, then the desire is to see that. If the goal is to increase graduation rates, decrease repeat pregnancies, decrease criminal justice system involvement, decrease recidivism, decrease suicide attempts, or increase school attendance, then these are what to be assessed.

Recognizing contributions is a mechanism to improve overall program outcomes. A straightforward approach to recognize contribution is through recognizing attendance. In order for participants to progress to overall program outcomes, it is important to participate in the programming that is tied to the outcome. Arguably, without participating in the programming, the outcome cannot be reached or it will take longer. As a result, recognizing and celebrating participation in the program are important mechanisms to pursue in order to increase the likelihood of improving program outcomes.

If a goal is to decrease pregnancies, then this should be measured. If the goal is to decrease the spread of sexually transmitted diseases, then this should be measured. If the goal is to decrease gun violence or gang involvement, then a link between the program and this outcome should be measured against the backdrop of the element of recognizing contributions through celebrations.

STRUCTURING CELEBRATIONS

Program celebrations can be structured in several ways. Some can be within the program itself through circles at openings or closings of regular program sessions. This can be done in the circle through statements such as "Today marks the return to the group of Diana" or "We want to recognize Trevor for how much he has added to the discussion today." Other comments can be to open the group to those who wish to share observations of contributions or compliments. Those can be presented such as: "We are opening up the circle to share positive observations of contributions to the program. Anyone who wishes to celebrate someone's contribution can do so now." It opens up the circle for participants and staff to share a positive comment, for example: "I want Maria to know that her ideas for how to go about recruiting new members were very helpful and have led us to start relying on social media postings more frequently."

Other ways to recognize contributions through celebration and crafting celebrity is dependent on budget. In the program described in the Lesson from the Circle of this chapter, four billboards were utilized. The billboards were located in four Chicago neighborhoods, including the neighborhood where the youth resided and where the program was housed. The billboard featured several participants in an advertisement that they created and was a reflection of their work in the program. This allowed the participants to witness how their work had impact and also provided public recognition of their work. It provided an opportunity for celebrity for the featured youth and those affiliated with the program. While not all programs will have the budget for a billboard, we raise this promotion as a possibility related to program planning and grant writing so that there is a possibility for it to be included. This chapter stresses importance of recognition. Regularized recognition and advanced planning to build recognition are stressed.

There are other opportunities to build in recognition. We do want to differentiate between recognition and incentives. Incentives are items or privileges utilized as exchange for achievement or participation. Recognition is tied to positive performance and is intended to encourage additional positive performance in the recipient and other participants. Recognition is intended to celebrate contribution but not to be specifically utilized as an exchange. Recognition is a form of an incentive; however, all incentives are not based on recognition.

Recognition is built on a foundation of contribution. Incentives can be built on contributions, yet our approach is to embed an internal locus of control to the participant to promote self-motivation. Incentives tend to be carrot (reward) focused, and making contributions is motivated by the desire for recognition. The goal with recognition is to show appreciation for behavior but not to condition behavior based only on the existence of an incentive.

Incentives such as gift cards for participation are rewards. Recognition, unlike an incentive, is not revealed in advance to motivate behavior. Arguably, motivation is easy to inspire through incentives. Consistency of contribution is challenging. Our experience is that recognition of contributions is more sustainable and leads to continued participation than traditional incentives based on attendance. We argue that verbal praise introduces a more interactive, human approach to programs. We also state that the recognition has more of an impact because it also has community components linked to outside of the program recognition. Verbal praise is important. In a society where there is growing public criticism, public praise is well placed with youth.

CHAPTER 10

Postprogram Follow-up

Lesson from the Circle
They are parents, managers, policy directors, truck drivers, higher education professionals, and real estate developers. Some even work in social services with youth programs. Now removed some 20 years after their initial involvement within the program, they are all on a Zoom meeting call on a Saturday night after the first month of the COVID-19 pandemic.

They initiated a "check-in" call with the former staff. They talked of life experiences, current issues, and stories from the program days, including trips they took with the program. They all knew what the others were up to prior to the call, having maintained contact with each other.

During the program, some were considered more "at risk" than others, but arguably, to a person, their lives were full and with meaning. There was laughter, tears of concern for loved ones during the pandemic, but most of all, they were happy to be "connected."

The program, called "Connextions," ended before the calendar year 2000, but for them, their involvement meant a lifetime of relationships, memories, and lessons learned from their experiences in the short time together. The staff instilled principles that would carry on for years, and beyond the ending celebration, was sure to keep an open eye and ear to their development.

LESSONS FROM THE LITERATURE

The youth programs discussed here, and any youth program for that matter, can have successes and failures concerning following up. Many programs are known to have successful outcomes while youth are involved in the program, only to have youth return to old behaviors after the program or adults in their lives are gone. This should not discourage youth providers

High Impact Practices with Urban Youth—Circles at the Center. Yan Dominic Searcy and Troy Harden,
Oxford University Press. © Oxford University Press 2023. DOI: 10.1093/oso/9780197549926.003.0010

from doing much needed work. Many young people, years removed from the programs they were involved in as adolescents, tell of how the things they learned and people that impacted them still have influence on their choices and decisions in the present. Research concerning adolescent brain development speak to the malleable nature of the brain, and that this time period is an important era for new learning and integration. As research on emerging adulthood has confirmed, the developmental processes, including physical and psychological development take place well into the 20s. It is important, then, for those who work with young people to recognize that, although it may not be clear on "what's next" for them, it is clear that their work can have change effects for the long term.

YOUTH TRANSITIONS: WHERE DO THEY GO?

Given the above, how do providers prepare young people for "lifelong lessons" that can occur during their stint in their programs, and how do we create infrastructure to support youth as they move on from their presence? Young people transition from high school and move on to a number of opportunities, challenges, and adventures. Many youth go to colleges and universities, while some go on to the military, trade school opportunities, and service ventures, such as the Peace Corp and AmeriCorps. However, in recent literature, many have written about the school-to-prison pipeline, suggesting that young people, particularly young people of color and those who come from low-income backgrounds, are tracked into prisons.

Although perhaps not an intention of educators and providers, the disproportionate numbers of Black and Latinx young men and women who end up in the criminal justice system suggests that something is happening that steers them away from the opportunities mentioned previously. For providers who work with these populations, the stakes can become increasingly high once the participants leave the program, and with the amount of young people who end up within the criminal justice system or, worse yet, harmed by the system, become a case of alarm, and leaving their programs can result in negative outcomes. In addition, young people who are still within child welfare systems age out of protective custody and often find themselves without necessary resources to survive and sustain, including housing, case management services, and educational opportunities. They become increasingly vulnerable to encounters with police and other harmful circumstances based on unstable environments and high-risk encounters. Given the myriad paths that our young people follow, how then do we develop our programs to grant viable skills and create an environment that prepares all youth to transition to the "next" in a good way? Let's discuss some of the best practices for how programs can create healthy transitions and also develop methods to support young people in their next stages of development.

PROGRAM CLOSURE AND TRANSITIONING

In clinical settings, a normalized component in ending clinical work is to invite discussions around transitioning out of therapy or the like and what this will mean for both the clinician and the person being seen. In addition, high schools often prepare their students to transition to college, and advisors create plans for college, including college tours, financial aid workshops, and assistance with applications. Major rituals of our society include high school graduations and proms; and "trunk parties," where family and community come together before people leave for college to give gifts related to housing and educational needs, are common.

Each spring and summer, social media posts are filled with pictures celebrating these events, and they serve as important communal markers for the transition from adolescence to adulthood. However, for many young people, these are not the norms. Young people who have struggled in high school, been pushed out into alternative schools, or who have unstable living environments often do not have clear paths, lack parental or commu- nity support, and struggle with the transition. Given that even those with the best circumstances, youth who do have a clear understanding of the path ahead as well as supports, still struggle with attachment and aban- donment concerns or may have parents or guardians with little knowledge of college or the military; young people could benefit from programs that help them transition to the next level in their development. Although the case can be made that some young people are "unprepared," many are "un- derprepared" and can benefit from added attention and resources at this stage. The next section addresses this and discusses best practices in clo- sure, including transitions, referral, and relationships.

"PASSAGES" VERSUS "TERMINATION"

"Termination" is a loaded word. Although it effectively demonstrates the finality of the programmatic relationship, it also implies "death," an ending with no physical future. Although clinically accepted, it does not speak to the many aspects of leaving a program or provider and transitioning to the next stage of development. For this purpose, we use the term *passages*. Borrowing from the term "rites of passage," passages can imply moving from one stage of life to the next. Rites of passage is a term established by Arnold Van Gennup over a century ago (1960) to describe what he saw as rituals designed to assist young people to move into adulthood. In studying several indigenous societies, Van Gennup noted that adults arranged intricate and intentional activities to prepare youth to transition to adulthood. Many of these activities took the form of rituals, or activities designed to reinforce important lessons and mark acknowledgment and affirmation of a young person's readiness to mature into adulthood.

The rituals, in this sense, were both "process" and "events," and some were private and closed off to the large community, and others were public with the expectation that family and community members would participate. In our modern world, high school graduation, or the event of high school graduation, is often referred to as a "spring rite of passage"; however, all young people have to do is "show up," and although highly ritualized, including common standards of conducting these events, including commencement speeches, handing diplomas, and turning tassels, there is little challenge or few lessons to establish preparation for the next stage. Technically, high school is supposed to have provided the challenges, but most providers know that young people often need more and thus the need for their programs. Preparing for this particular passage becomes more important than the ritual marking the passage. With this, the meaning making behind this can be more involved and intentional, and young people can be better prepared. In this vein, young people can truly be "passengers" traveling from one stage to the next, recognizing there will be many opportunities to move from one stage of life to the next with intention, grace, and vision.

INITIATING THE CONVERSATION

Prior to beginning the passage, staff can begin to address the key components that their young people have gained and what they may still need at the next step. This can include skills and knowledge that they have learned in the program, the individualized needs of each young person, and resources that either the program has or that young people can be connected to. An honest assessment of this can lead to a fair discussion of what your program can do and cannot do for the participants.

Once assets and limitations have been addressed, staff can then explore what the transition means to them. Many youth have experienced poor transitions in their lives. People come and go without warning, programs close without transparency, and many people end up in new ventures unprepared or ill-informed without adequate preparation. The lack of experience can lead to difficulty with transitions of people, and at times, workers can have their own difficulties with the youth. These can include difficulty initiating program closure, detaching from young people and staff to avoid uncomfortable feelings, clinging to young people, or adopting a "savior" identity that sends the message to young people that they may not have any other valuable adults or resources beyond the staff. Programs can do well to discuss "termination styles" with staff, assessing barriers and strengths to creating closure for the youth.

Once this has been addressed, staff are ready to begin the important process of preparing for the next steps for the youth. The initial conversation can discuss clearly acknowledging the passage stage, including what young people may have accomplished, how they can still develop, and what the timeline of events and/or activities can include. The timeline is important, as it gives young people clarity concerning what they can expect, what needs they may have prior to the passage, and how staff can assist and support with the next phase.

The participants can be involved actively in this process and invited to establish what areas they can engage, including plans for themselves, supporting other participants, planning for events, and even how they may like to either stay connected or involved as time goes on. Some high schools only invite young people who are already highly involved to participate in closing processes, including student government leaders, yearbook volunteers, and valedictorian and speakers. The opportunity here is to involve ALL youth, giving several young people roles in determining their processes for closure. Thus, this is not only something happening to them, but also something they are creating, including planning and implementing. Once the timeline has been established and planning for activities and events have begun, youth workers can address and build in activities that support the lifelong journey.

CELEBRATION AND CEREMONY

The final events can include anything, including celebration activities that highlight youth achievement. These can include small events that include only youth and staff or public events where youth can be acknowledged and affirmed. Questions for providers to consider include the following:

- What are the assets of your program related to helping young people transition to their next stage (people, activities, knowledge, skills, fiscal resources, etc.)?
- What are the limitations of your program? (Where do you need assistance? Who do you refer to?)
- Where can they turn outside of you and your program?
- What conversation(s) do you need to have with your participants?
- When do you want these to take place?
- What events do you have planned to mark their passage?
- How will you stay in touch with the young people?
- What processes or structures do you have to maintain contact or supportive ties?

OPPORTUNITIES FOR FUTURE ENGAGEMENT

When a young person enters our program, we see all the challenges they possess, as well as their potential. It is hoped by now the program has allowed them to see the things that you see in them, including the barriers to their development and their strengths. However, as many of us know, and as Mike Tyson says: "Everyone has a plan until they get hit in the mouth!" How, then, do we prepare young people for the inevitable ups and downs of life? By now, you have established that there is at least one caring person in their life (it is hoped there are several!). We hope the relationships in the program have been great and, in many cases, life changing, but how will they know how to identify other trusting adults who can support them on their way? Let's discuss social capital for a moment.

Social capital can be defined as the trustworthy relationships we build that can gain us support, resources, and opportunities for success. It is built on normative behavior between these relationships, where individuals can be comfortable in the accountability and expectations of the relationship. An example of this is when someone asks for a job referral to a company that you may be connected to. If you know this person as reliable or know the different strengths that this person possesses, one can feel comfortable making the connection, understanding the value between the different parties. A famous saying is that it's not what you know, it's who you know. However, in Chicago, a variation of this is not who you know, but who sent you. If I trust and value the person who sent you, then I know that you carry the same values or "norms" of this person, and I thus can trust that you will operate in a trustworthy manner. For young people who come from historically marginalized backgrounds, this can be fraught with challenges.

Researchers have pointed to the often embedded and close relationships that many people have in marginalized communities. Although these ties may be close and trustworthy for them, they do not always have connections to greater resources beyond their neighborhoods. Their networks are dense, and the opportunities to connect with the rest of the world are few. Many of us know the stories of about the young person who has never traveled beyond the confines of his environment, feeling out of place in new settings where people do not look, think, or act like them. The temptation is to stay connected to the familiar. The youth worker can stand as an important bridge for the young person, giving them access to a world beyond their previous possibilities. However, a youth worker who mistrusts the larger world and struggles with the same temptations as the youth can fail to make those valuable connections.

One example of a program is one where the youth workers were intentional about showing young people beyond their environment, scheduling trips to different locations, including out of state and, in some cases, internationally, to expose youth to a new world. The intent was to ensure that the young people knew that their worlds were not limited to their neighborhoods, that although their communities had value, they could learn from others and other places, and if they chose, return with new ideas, new possibilities, and new relationships.

When the activities mentioned above are done well, we have seen where the young people involved in our programs have maintained a sense of connection to not only the program, but also the values, principles, and relationships that they have encountered. Far beyond a program, they become *high impact persons*, committed to not only demonstrating the lessons they have learned, but also impacting the lives of others, including youth who were once like them. We hope in this book you will not only have read about practices that will support your working with young people, but the stories that bring these practices to life. After all, it is the stories, the relationships with youth and their families and loved ones that stay with us through the years and remind us of why we do the work that we do.

EPILOGUE

Rocket Science

We resent the popular conception of rocket science. Rocket science is a popular refrain utilized as if that discipline is the most difficult of vocational activities. Rocket scientists benefit from computer-aided modeling, running equations based on established mathematical constants, and the ability to run multiple simulations. Even when actual rockets incinerate or crash during development, we hear that those were actual successes. There is no such luxury in working with youth. There is no such luxury in working with people. We are unpredictable. Our own behavior has surprised us. Our mathematical constant is change. Crashes in youth development can be fatal. The most difficult of vocational activities is working with people.

So, we caution that while we provide perspective and insight, we know that the work will remain challenging and unpredictable. Technology advancements and social media dynamics also contribute to the challenges. But, what we provide is intended to lessen the challenge and the unpredictability.

This book is ultimately about sharing. We want to share our lessons from the circle as we see a new generation of youth workers emerge. We saw that progress and new perspective are occurring, but we also saw that some common errors are still being made. We also saw that some looked to us for direction, and we wanted to make sure that the knowledge was not lost.

Youth work is challenging and draining. But youth work is also supremely rewarding and renewing. We share out of humility that we do not know it all. We share out of humility offering what we do know. The circle at the center is what we do know has been effective with connecting with youth and improving outcomes. The circle creates an environment that supports and affirms. It provides a place for emotional and physical safety.

We are encouraged. It's not rocket science.

NOTES

CHAPTER 5
1. Issues such as these present ethical issues, including obligations for mandated reporters, group confidentiality, and concern to minimize potential harm. Connecting with organizational leaders, street outreach members, and mandated reporting anonymous hotlines can always assist with ascertaining appropriate steps in situations such as this. Providers should consult guidelines offered by their organizations, city, and state in order to ascertain appropriate steps.

BIBLIOGRAPHY

INTRODUCTION

Hampton, R. (2019). Which People? How People of Color Evolved from a Gesture of Solidarity and Respect to a Cover for Avoiding the Complexities of Race. *Slate*, February 13. https://slate.com/human-interest/2019/02/people-of-color-phrase-history-racism.html.

Malesky, K. (2014). The Journey from "Colored" to "Minorities" to "People of Color." *Code Switch, NPR*, March 30. https://www.npr.org/sections/codeswitch/2014/03/30/295931070/the-journey-from-colored-to-minorities-to-people-of-color.

Yeager, K. A., and Bauer-Wu, S. M. (2013). Cultural Humility: Essential Foundation for Clinical Researchers. *Applied Nursing Research* 26:4.

CHAPTER 1

Backer, T. E., and Guerra, N. G. (2011). Evidence-Based Practices in Youth Violence Prevention: The State of the Art. *American Journal of Community Psychology* 48:31–42.

Barton, A. C., and Tan, E. (2010). We Be Burnin'! Agency, Identity, and Science Learning. *Journal of the Learning Sciences* 19(2):187–229. http://www.jstor.org/stable/27801116

Boyes-Watson, C. (2005). Seeds of Change: Using Peacemaking Circles to Build a Village for Every Child. *Child Welfare* 84(2):191–208.

Cater, M., Machtmes, K., and Fox, J. E. (2013). A Phenomenological Examination of Context on Adolescent Ownership and Engagement Rationale. *Qualitative Report* 04–22.

Dioum Kelly, D. (2016). The Power of Traditional African Healing Methods. https://chopra.com/articles/the-power-of-traditional-african-healing-methods.

Greenwood, P. (2010). *Preventing and Reducing Youth Crime and Violence: Using Evidence-Based Practices*. Sacramento, CA: Governor's Office of Gang and Youth Violence Policy.

Harano, E. (2017). Design+Participation+Ownership: An Exploration of the Possibilities of Youth-Adult Curricular Co-design. https://medium.com/erika-harano/design-ownership-participation-f72e8f50d498.

Kovach, M. (2009). *Indigenous Methodologies: Characteristics, Conversations, and Contexts*. Toronto: University of Toronto Press.

Krauss, S. E., Collura, J., Zeldin, S., Ortega, A., Abdullah, H., and Sulaiman, A. H. (2014). Youth-Adult Partnership: Exploring Contributions to Empowerment,

Agency and Community Connections in Malaysian Youth Programs. *Journal of Youth and Adolescence* 43(9):1550–1562.

Kuh, G. (2008). *High-Impact Educational Practices: What They Are, Who Has Access to Them, and Why They Matter.* American Association of Colleges and Universities Press.

Larson, R., and Angus, R. (2011). Adolescents' Development of Skills for Agency in Youth Programs: Learning to Think Strategically. *Child Development* 82(1):277–294.

Levine, B., and Gallogly, V. G. (1985). *Group Therapy with Alcoholics: Outpatient and Inpatient Approaches.* Thousand Oaks, CA: Sage.

Linnenbrink, E. A., and Pintrich, P. R. (2003). The Role of Self-Efficacy Beliefs in Student Engagement and Learning in the Classroom. *Reading and Writing Quarterly* 19:119–137.

Mantooth, L., and Hamilton, P. (2004). *4-H Service Learning Standard and Best Practice Guide.* Knoxville, TN: University of Tennessee.

Mehl-Madrona, L., and Mainguy, B. (2014). Introducing Healing Circles and Talking Circles into Primary Care. *Permanente Journal,* 18(2):4.

Miller, A. L., Williams, L. M., and Silberstein, S. M. (2018). Found My Place: The Importance of Faculty Relationships for Seniors' Sense of Belonging. *Higher Education Research and Development,* November, 38(3):594–608.

Pranis, K., Wedge, M., and Stuart, B. (2003). *Peacemaking Circles.* Living Justice Press.

Ryan, R. M., and Deci, E. L. (2000). Self-Determination Theory and the Facilitation of Intrinsic Motivation, Social Development, and Well-Being. *American Psychologist* 55(1):68–78.

Smith, L. T. (2012). *Decolonizing Methodologies: Research and Indigenous Peoples.* Zed Books.

Strayhorn, T. L. (2019). *College Students' Sense of Belonging: A Key to Educational Success for All Students.* 2nd ed. Routledge, Taylor & Francis Group.

Toseland, R. W., and Horton, H. (2013). *Group Work, Encyclopedia of Social Work.* NASW and Oxford University Press.

Wilson, S. (2008). *Research Is Ceremony.* Fernwood Publishing.

CHAPTER 2

Bausman, M. (2012). HSBE Course of Study—Human Behavior in the Social Environment. https://libguides.library.hunter.cuny.edu/c.php?g=438857&p=2991442.

Bean, C. B., Harlow, M., and Forneris, T. (2016). Examining the Importance of Supporting Youth's Basic Needs in One Youth Leadership Programme: A Case Study Exploring Programme Quality. *International Journal of Adolescence and Youth* 22(2):195–209.

Bilet, T., Olsen, T., Andersen, J. R., and Martinsen, E. W. (2020). Cognitive Behavioral Group Therapy for Panic Disorder in a General Clinical Setting: A Prospective Cohort Study with 12 to 31 Years Follow-up. *BMC Psychiatry* 20(1):1–7.

Bronfenbrenner, U. (1979). *The Ecology of Human Development.* Cambridge, MA: Harvard University Press.

Dulmus, C., and Sowers, K. (2012). *Social Work Fields of Practice: Historical Trends, Professional Issues, and Future Opportunities.* New York: Wiley.

Ellardus Van Zyl, L., and Stander, M. (2014). Flourishing Interventions: A Practical Guide to Student Development. In *Psycho-social Career Meta-capacities,* edited

by M. Coetzee, 265–276. Cham, Switzerland: Springer. https://doi.org/
10.1007/978-3-319-00645-1_14.

Eriksson, M., Ghazinour, M., and Hammarstrom, A. (2018). Different Uses of
Bronfenbrenner's Ecological Theory in Public Mental Health Research: What Is
Their Value for Guiding Public Mental Health Policy and Practice? *Social Theory
& Health* 16.

Garst, B., Scheider, I., and Baker, D. (2001). Outdoor Adventure Program
Participation Impacts on Adolescent Self-Perception. *Journal of Experiential
Education* 24(1):41–49.

Kells, M., et al. (2019). Engaging Youth (Adolescents and Young Adults) to Change
Frequent Marijuana Use: Motivational Enhancement Therapy (MET in Primary
Care). *Journal of Pediatric Nursing* 49.

Keyes, C. (2002). The Mental Health Continuum: From Languishing to Flourishing in
Life. *Journal of Health and Social Behavior* 43(2).

Kwong, T. Y., and Hayes, D. K. (2017). Adverse Family Experiences and Flourishing
Amongst Children Ages 6–17 Years: 2011/12 National Survey of children's
Health. *Child Abuse and Neglect* 70:240–246.

Lipsey, A. F., et al. (2020). Evaluation of First-Person Storytelling on Changing
Health-Related Attitudes, Knowledge, Behaviors, and Outcomes: A Scoping
Review. *Patient Education & Counseling* 103(10):1922–1934.

Melles, M. O.., and Ricker, C. L. (2017). Youth Participation in HIV and Sexual and
Reproductive Health Decision-Making, Policies, Programmes: Perspectives
from the Field. *International Journal of Adolescence and Youth* 23(2):159–167.

Schotanus-Dijkstra, M., ten Klooster, P. M., Drossaert, C. H. C., Ten Klooster, P., and
Marijke Schotanus-Dijkstra, M. (2016). Validation of the Flourishing Scale
in a Sample of People with Suboptimal Levels of Mental Well-Being. *BMC
Psychology* 4:12.

Schultz, K., et al. (2016). Key Roles of Community Connectedness in Healing from
Trauma. *Psychology of Violence* 6(1):42–48.

Seligman, M. (2011). *Flourish: A Visionary New Understanding of Happiness and Well-
being*. Simon and Schuster.

Torok, M., et al. (2019). Preventing Adolescent Suicide: A Systematic Review of the
Effectiveness and Change Mechanisms of Suicide Prevention Gatekeeping
Training Programs for Teachers and Parents. *Journal of Adolescence* 73:100–112.

Van Wormer, K., and Besthorn, F. (2017). *Human Behavior and the Social Environment,
Macro Level*. Oxford University Press.

Venning, A., Wilson, A., Kettler, L., and Elliot, J. (2012). Mental Health among Youth
in South Australia: A Survey of Flourishing, Languishing, Struggling, and
Floundering. *Australian Psychological Society* 48:299–310.

Walker, D., Pereznieto, P., Bergh, G., and Smith, K. (2014). *Partners for Change: Young
People and Governance in a post-2015 World*. London: Overseas Development
Institute. http://restlessdevelopment.org/file/partners-for-change-full-report-
amended-pdf.

Wang, M., and Fredricks, J. (2014). The Reciprocal Links between School Engagement,
Youth Problem Behaviors, and School Dropout during Adolescence. *Child
Development* 85(2).

Werner, O., Abassi, H., Lavastre, K., Guillaumont, S., Picot, M. C., Serrand, C., Dulac,
Y., et al. (2019). Factors Influencing the Participation of Adolescents and Young
Adults with a Congenital Heart Disease in a Transition Education Program:

A Prospective Multicentre Controlled Study. *Patient Education and Counseling* 102(12):2223–2230.

Wiley, R. (2016). A Case Study of Cognitive Processing Therapy for a Military Medic with Posttraumatic Stress Disorder. *Journal of Cognitive Psychotherapy* 30(3).

Wilkinson, C., et al. (2017). Cognitive Processing Therapy for Post-traumatic Stress Disorder in a University Counselling Center: An Outcome Study. *Cognitive Behaviour Therapist* 10:E20.

Wilson, G., et al. (2018). The Use of Eye-Movement Desensitization Reprocessing (EMDR) Therapy in Treating Post-traumatic Stress Disorder—A Systematic Narrative Review. *Frontiers in Psychology* 9:923.

Witten, H., et al. (2019). Adolescent Flourishing: A Systematic Review. *Cogent Psychology* 6.

Woods-Jaeger, B., et al. (2020). Building a Contextually-Relevant Understanding of Resilience among African American Youth Exposed to Community Violence. *Behavioral Medicine* 2020:46(3–4).

CHAPTER 3

Avolio, B., and Wernsing, T. S. (2008). *Practicing Authentic Leadership*.

Azanza, G., Moriano, J. A., and Molero, F. (2013). Authentic Leadership and Organizational Culture as Drivers of Employees' Job Satisfaction. *Revista de Psicología del Trabajo y de las Organizaciones* 29(2):45–50.

DeVera, M., Corpus, J. E., and Ramos, D. D. (2016). Towards Understanding a Multi-stakeholder Approach in a Youth Leadership Development Program. *International Journal of Public Leadership* 12(2):143–153.

Eddy, P. L., and VanDerLinden, K. E. (2006). Emerging Definitions of Leadership in Higher Education. *Community College Review* 34(1).

Fraser, S. (2014). Authentic Leadership in Higher Education: Influencing the Development of Future Leaders. Education doctoral. Paper 187.

Fredericka, H. R., Wood, J. A., West, G. R., and Winston, B. E. (2016). The Effect of the Accountability Variables of Responsibility, Openness, and Answerability on Authentic Leadership. *Journal of Research on Christian Education* 25(3):302–316.

Gallagher, E. (2002). Leadership: A Paradigm Shift. *Management in Education* 16(3):24–29.

Gardner, W. L., Cogliser, C. C., Davis, K. M., and Dickens, M. P. (2011). Authentic Leadership: A Review of the Literature and Research Agenda. *Leadership Quarterly* 22:1120–1145.

Giordano-Mulligan, M., and Eckardt, S. (2019). Nurses' Perception of Authentic Nurse Leader Attributes. *Nursing Administration Quarterly* 43(2):164–174.

Iachini, A., et al. (2017). Maximizing the Contribution of After-School Programs to Positive Youth Development: Exploring Leadership and Implementation within Girls on the Run. *Children & Schools* 39(1):43–51.

Jensen, S. M., and Luthans, F. (2006). Relationship between Entrepreneurs' Psychological Capital and Their Authentic Leadership. *Journal of Managerial Issues* 18(2):254–273.

Kinsler, L. (2014). Born to Be Me. Who Am I Again? The Development of Authentic Leadership Using Evidence-Based Leadership Coaching and Mindfulness. International Coaching Psychology Review 9(1):92–105.

Kotterman, J. (2006). Leadership versus Management: What's the Difference? Journal for Quality and Participation, 29(2):13–17.

Larson, R. W., Izenstark, D., Rodriguez, G., and Perry, S. C. (2016). The Art of Restraint: How Experienced Program Leaders Use Their Authority to Support Youth Agency. *Journal of Research on Adolescence* 26(4):845–863.

Laschinger, H. K., and Fida, R. (2014). New Nurses' Burnout and Workplace Wellbeing: The Influence of Authentic Leadership and Psychological Capital. *Burnout Research* 19–28 (Original source: https://prothesiswriter.com/sub-samples/influence-of-authentic-leadership-and-empowerment-on-nursing-staff-retention.)

Laws, J. (2016). Keys to Employee Engagement. *Occupational Health & Safety.* 85(6):44–45.

Leedy, G., and Smith, J. (2012). Development of Emotional Intelligence in First-Year Undergraduate Students in a Frontier State. *College Student Journal*, 46(4):795–804.

Luthans, F., and Avolio, B. J. (2003). Authentic Leadership Development. In *Positive Organizational Scholarship: Foundations of a New Discipline*, edited by K. S. Caneribm, J. E. Dutton, and R. E. Quinns. San Francisco: Berrett-Koehler.

Manolis, J., et al. (2009). Leadership: A New Frontier in Conservation Science. *Conservation Biology* August.

Miranda, A. O., and Goodman, E. D. (1996). Similarities between Social Interest and Contemporary Definitions of Corporate Leadership. *Individual Psychology: The Journal of Adlerian Theory, Research & Practice* 52(3):261–270.

Mortensen, J., Lichty, L., Foster-Fishman, P., Harfst, S., Warsinske, K., and Abdullah, K. (2014). Leadership through a Youth Lens: Understanding Youth Conceptualizations of Leadership. *Journal of Community Psychology* 42(4):447–462. https://doi.org/10.1002/jcop.21620.

Neider, L. L., and Schriesheim, C. A. (2011). The Authentic Leadership Inventory (ALI): Development and Empirical Tests. *Leadership Quarterly* 22(6):1146–1164. https://doi.org/10.1016/j.leaqua.2011.09.008.

Papen, U., and Thériault, V. (2017). Writing Retreats as a Milestone in the Development of PhD Students' Sense of Self as Academic Writers. *Studies in Continuing Education* https://doi.org/10.1080/0158037X.2017.1396973.

Roberts, C. (2008). Leadership and Gender: Spiderman Meets Charlotte's Web. *Journal of the Indiana Academy of the Social Sciences* 12:36–45.

Tate, T. F. (2003). Servant Leadership for Schools and Youth Programs. *Reclaiming Children and Youth* 12(1):33–39.

Walumbwa, F. O., Avolio, B. J., Gardner, W. L., Wersing, T. S., and Peterson, S. J. (2008). Authentic Leadership: Development and Validation of a Theory-Based Measure. *Journal of Management* 34(1):89–126.

CHAPTER 4

Bertrand, M., Brooks, M. D., and Dominguez, A. (2020). Challenging Adultism: Centering Youth as Decision-makers. *Urban Education.* https://doi.org/10.1177/0042085920959135.

Bettencourt, G. M. (2018). Embracing Problems, Processes, and Contact Zones: Using Youth Participatory Action Research to Challenge Adultism. *Action Research* 18(2):153–170. https://doi.org/10.1177/1476750318789475.

DeJong, K., and Love, B. J. (2015). Youth Oppression as a Technology of Colonialism: Conceptual Frameworks and Possibilities for Social Justice Education Praxis. *Equity & Excellence in Education* 48(3):489–508. https://doi.org/10.1080/10665684.2015.1057086.

Fine, M. (1995). The Politics of Whose "At-Risk." In *Children and Families "At-Promise"*. edited by B. B. Swadener and S. Lubek. New York: SUNY Press.

Gadsden, V. L., and Dixon-Román, E. J. (2017). "Urban" Schooling and "Urban" Families: The Role of Context and Place. *Urban Education* 52(4):431–459. https://doi.org/10.1177/0042085916652189.

Gillard, A., and Witt, P. (2008). Recruitment and Retention in Youth Programs. *Journal of Park and Recreational Administration* 26(2):177–188. http://www2.wiu.edu/users/ps114/articles/Recruitment_and_Retention_in_Youth_Progr ams.pdf.

Scales, P. C., Benson, P. L., Oesterle, S., Hill, K., Hawkins, J. D., and Pashak, T. J. (2016). The Dimensions of Successful Young Adult Development: A Conceptual and Measurement Framework. *Applied Developmental Science* 20(3):150–174. https://doi.org/10.1080/10888691.2015.1082429.

Toldson, I. A. (2019). Why It's Wrong to Label Students "At-Risk." *The Conversation*. https://theconversation.com/why-its-wrong-to-label-students-at-risk-109621.

Vega, S., Glynn-Crawford, H., and Van-Pelt, J.-L. (2012). Safe Schools for LGBTQI Students: How Do Teachers View Their Role in Promoting Safe Schools? *Equity & Excellence in Education* 45(2):250–260. https://doi.org/10.1080/10665 684.2012.671095.

Wogan, J. B. (2015). My Brother's Keeper Is Great, But What About the girls? Governing. https://www.governing.com/archive/gov-brothers-keeper-black-girls-obama.html.

CHAPTER 5

Blanchet-Cohen, N., and Brunson, L. (2014). Creating Settings for Youth Empowerment and Leadership: An Ecological Perspective. *Child & Youth Services* 35:216–236. https://doi.org/10.1080/0145935X.2014.938735.

Jennings, L., et al. (2006). Toward a Critical Social Theory of Youth Empowerment. *Journal of Community Practice* 14:31–55. https://doi.org/10.1300/J125v1 4n01_03.

CHAPTER 6

Meunier, P. (2020). What Makes a Great Youth Worker? The Professional Youth Worker. https://training.yipa.org/blog/what-makes-for-great-youth-workers/.

CHAPTER 8

Fiddler, C. (2008). Retreats Bring Youth Back to Their Roots. *Windspeaker* 26(1):26.

Gartner-Manzon, S., and Giles, A. R. (2018). Lasting impacts of an Aboriginal youth leadership retreat: a case study of Alberta's Future Leaders Program. *Journal of Adventure Education & Outdoor Learning* 18(4):338–352.

Guanci, G., and Medeiros, M. (2018). Shared governance Strategic Planning Retreat: A Best Practice. *Nursing Management* 49(8):36–40.

Huberman, A. (2020). Change Your Brain: Neuroscientist Andrew Huberman, *Rich Roll Podcast*, July 20 https://www.richroll.com/podcast/andrew-huber man-533/.

Jacobson, A. (2021). The Highest Bidder. *JAMA*. 325(1):27–28.

Knox, J. (2016). The Monastic Movement: Origins & Purposes. *World History Encyclopedia*. https://www.worldhistory.org/article/930/the-monastic-movem ent-origins--purposes/ World History Encyclopedia.

Taranova, Y. (2010). Old-Style Bureaucracy Stymies Pro-Kremlin Youth Retreat. *New York Times*, July 6, 159.

Tori, C. D. (1999). Change on Psychological Scales Following Buddhist and Roman Catholic Retreats. *Psychological Reports* 84(1):125.

Treleaven, S. (2019). The Enduring Appeal of Escapism: A History of Wellness Retreats. Medium. https://elemental.medium.com/the-obsession-with-welln ess-retreats-goes-back-centuries-5c491cf2baa3.

CHAPTER 9

Craig, W. (2017). 3 Reasons Why Employee Recognition Will Always Matter. *Forbes*, July 17. https://www.forbes.com/sites/williamcraig/2017/07/17/3-reasons-why-employee-recognition-will-always-matter/?sh=797f401863c9.

Gardner, L. A., Vella, S. A., and Magee, C. A. (2018). The Role of Implicit Beliefs and Achievement Goals as Protective Factors in Youth Sport. *Journal of Applied Sport Psychology* 30(1):83–95.

Law, B. M., Siu, A. M.. H., and Shek, D. T.L, (2012). Recognition for Positive Behavior as a Critical Youth Development Construct: Conceptual Bases and Implications on Youth Service Development. *Scientific World Journal* 2012:7.

Searcy, Yan. (2007). Placing the Horse in Front of the Wagon: Toward a Conceptual Understanding of the Development of Self-Esteem in Children and Adolescents. *Child and Adolescent Social Work Journal* 24(2):121–131.

Skinner, B. F. (1953). *Science and Human Behavior*. New York: Macmillan.

Talent Development. 69(4):108–109. 2p. 1.

Terryberry.com. (2021). Employee Recognition. terryberry.com.

White, P. (2015). *Improving Staff Morale through Authentic Appreciation*.

CHAPTER 10

Van Gennup, A. (1960*). The Rites of Passage*. 2nd ed. Chicago: University of Chicago Press.

INDEX

For the benefit of digital users, indexed terms that span two pages (e.g., 52–53) may, on occasion, appear on only one of those pages.

celebrity/celebrations (*cont.*)
  productivity/youth recognition
    benefits, 82
  program outcome benefits, 86
  retention benefits, 82–83
  T-shirts/wearable items approach, 82
  use of in circles, 13
  youth programming benefits, xii, 80–81
check-in. *See* opening check-in
    (discussion circles); PIES (physically,
    intellectually, emotionally,
    spiritually) check-in
circle at the center, defined, 16
circles. *See also* discussion circles
  approach to theory of, 13–14
  behavioral programming, 8
  Boyes-Watson on, 9
  centrality to HIPs, 6–7
  centrality to youth programming, 10–11
  communication of egalitarianism by,
    42
  discussion circles, 6–7
  goals of, 10–11
  group work vs., 8–9
  indigenous origin of, 7
  links to youth development, 8
  opening check-in, 40–42
  postprogram follow-up, 89–95
  role of sustained adult-youth
    participation, 18
  support role of, 14
  therapeutic applications of, 13
client-centered approaches, 6–7
cognitive evaluation theory, 5
cognitive processing therapy (CPT), 13
community
  as a created emotional space, 16
  ownership and, 4
  recruitment resources, 32
contributional leadership, 60–61, 63–65
COVID-19 pandemic, 37, 68, 89
Cs (competence, confidence, connection,
    character, caring/compassion), of
    positive youth development, 36–37
cultural humility, ix
curriculum
  allowance for/lessons in failure, 63
  approaches to building, viii
  atmosphere/physical space
    considerations, 55–56, 58

comparative importance of, 6
crafting content before, 3, 50–58
curriculum building, viii
elements in making choices, 55
outcome/impact considerations, 56
PIE and, 11–12
process vs. content ("what" vs.
    "how"), 53
role of active participation, 61
Search Institute's development
    assets, 35–36, 53

Department of Justice, 51
discussion circles, 39–49
  affirming participation, 45–46
  "blessing" of participants, 45
  closure, 49
  crafting ground rules, 42
  equity in participation, 46–47
  holding safe space for emotional
    sharing, 44–45
  listening and feedback, 47–49
  opening check-in, 40–42
  participant power sharing
    opportunties, 44

e-boards (youth executive boards), 62
EBPs. *See* evidence-based practices
emotional abuse, 37
emotional intelligence, 26
equity in participation (discussion
    circles), 46–47
events (public events). *See also* celebrity/
    celebrations
  allowing time for, 27
  importance of, 79–88
  relationship-building benefits, 29
  use as retention incentive, 37
evidence-based practices (EBPs)
  advantages of, 52
  application to HIPs, 2
  clinical trials, 51
  comments on implementation
    of, 8–9
  description, x, 51
  evaluation questions, 52
  HIPS as educational EBPs, 2
  leadership development skills, 43–44
  power sharing with adult staff, 43–44
  types of, 51

eye movement desensitization and
reprocessing (EMDR) therapy, 13

Facebook, 33
facilitators. *See also* youth practitioners
    availability trait of, 26
    description, 18
    hierarchy of authority and, 18
    importance of listening in discussion
        circles, 47–49
    need for authenticity by, ix
    at retreats, 76
    role in check-in tone setting, 40–42
    role in holding safe space for
        emotional sharing, 44–45
    role in maintaining respect, 40
    role in participant ownership of topic
        agendas, 43–44
    values/skills/talents requirements,
        56–57
flourishing (youth flourishing), x–xi
    centrality of circles to, 12
    importance of, 14–15
    indicators of resilience, 15–16
    role of focusing on leadership, 16–18
    Seligman's definition of, 14
    subjective well-being and, 14
Flourish (Seligman), 14
formal leadership, 60–62
Fraser, S., 23
Fredericka, H. R., 27–28
front-line practitioners, viii
Full Circle program, 79–80

Gardner, W. L., 82–83
G Herbo (rapper), 16
Gillard, A., 36
Goleman, Daniel, 26
graffiti, 4
Greenwood, P., 8–9
ground rules (discussion circles), 42
group work
    circles vs., 8–9
    defined, 8
    framing of, viii
Guerra, N. G., 8–9

Harano, E., 4–5
high impact practices (HIPs)
    application of EBPs to, 2

circles and, 14–16
description, 2
higher education HIPS, 2
links to program participation, 3
reasons for impact of, 4
role of self-exploration, 3
theoretical basis of program design,
    ix–x
with urban youth, 3
high-risk youth, 34–36
HIPs. *See* high impact practices

informal leadership, 60–61, 66
informed caring, viii
Instagram, 33

Jennings, L., 44

Keyes, C., 14
Krauss, S., 6

Lakota Sioux ethnic group, 7
Larson, R., 6, 22
Latino/Latinx students, 44, 59, 68,
    90–91
Law, B. M., 80–81
leadership
    agency and, 22
    approaches to showing care, 26–27
    availability to participants/staff,
        25–26
    building of confidence in, 28
    contributional leadership, 60–61,
        63–65
    creating opportunities for, 60–61
    definition, 21
    formal leadership, 60–62
    gaining participation through, 16–18
    importance of authenticity, 22–24
    including youth in decision-making,
        24–25
    informal leadership, 60–61, 66
    program components, 17
    project management, 60–61, 63, 64
    recommendations, 66–67
    recruitment, 64–65
    representational leadership, 60–61, 65
    role of active participation, 61
    role of inclusiveness, 24–25
    servant leadership, 21–22

leadership (*cont.*)
staff liaison positions, 62
traits of, 21–22
youth advisory boards, 60–61, 62
youth executive boards (e-board), 62
leadership focused retreats, 69
LGBTQI (lesbian, gay, bisexual,
transgender, queer/ questioning,
intersex) youth, 34
Linnenbrink, E. A., 5

Meek Mill (rapper), 16
Melles, M. O., 18, 19
mental health concerns, ix
Mexican students, 2
Miller, A. L., 3
Mortensen, J., 22
motivational enhancement therapy, 13
"My Brother's Keeper" (MBK) initiative,
34–35

National Institute of Mental Health, 51
North American Native Americans, 7

Obama, Barack, 34–35
opening check-in (discussion circles),
40–42
example, 40–41
goals of, 40, 41
PIES check-in, 41
tone setting role of, 41–42
outcome-focused retreats, 70
ownership
agency and, 6, 43–44
approaches to developing, 42, 44–45,
70
description/perspectives, 5–6
discussion circle ground rules, 42
Harano on, 4–5
by participants of topic agendas,
42–44
program planning and, 5–6
representational leadership and, 65

person-in-environment (PIE) theory,
11–12
description, ix–xi, 11–12
environmental component of, 12
reason for using circles with, 12,
13–14

varying predictions/explanations,
11–12
physical abuse, 53–54
PIES (physically, intellectually,
emotionally, spiritually) check-in, 41
Pintrich, P. R., 5
political retreats, 69
postprogram follow-up, 89–95
assets/limitations assessments, 92–
93, 94
Black/Latinx outcomes, 90–91
final celebration events, 93
future engagement opportunities,
94–95
"passages" vs. "termination," 91–92
possible youth transitions, 90
program closure/transitioning, 91
successes/failures of programs, 89–90
post-traumatic stress disorder (PTSD),
16
power sharing opportunities, 43–44
pregnancy, unwanted, ix
project management, 60–61, 63, 64
psychoanalysis, 13
Puerto Rican students, 2

recruitment, 30–38
accessibility considerations, 32
challenges/strategies, 30–31
community resources, 32
contributional leadership and, 64–65
determining target groups, 31
of high-risk youth, 33–36
incentives/role of family, 37
marketing plan development, 33
program capacity assessment, 31
program competition considerations,
32
retention recommendations, 36
risk vs. asset-based assessment, 33–32
role of five Cs of positive youth
development, 36–37
representational leadership, 60–61, 65
retreats, 68–78
attendance/staffing, 76
benefits of celebrity/celebrations,
82–83
elements for inclusion, 74–75
elements in planning, 69–70
ground rules, 75

historical background, 69
impact of, 69
importance of, xi–xii
length determination, 73–74
location choice, 71–72
pacing, 75
planning, 77–78
reasons for/goal setting, 70–71
role of facilitators, 76
timing of, 72–73
types/focus of, 57, 69, 70, 72
Ricker, C. L., 18, 19
rites of passage, 91–92

Schultz, K., 16
Search Institute, development assets,
35–36, 53
self-determination theory, 5
Seligman, M., 14
servant leadership, 21–22
sexual abuse, 53–54
sexually transmitted diseases, ix
Skinner, B. F., 80–81
Smith L. T., 7
Snapchat, 33
social media, 25, 33, 77
social work theory, micro-/mesosystem
levels, 13
spiritually-related retreats, 69
strategic planning retreats, 69
substance abuse, ix
Substance Abuse and Mental Health
Services Administration
(SAMHSA), 51

tagging, 4
Tan, E., 6
Tate, T. F., 21–22

theory
circles' approach to, 13–14
cognitive evaluation theory, 5
description, 11
person-in-environment, ix–x, 11–12
self-determination theory, 5
TikTok, 33
Twitter, 33

U.S. Census Bureau, ix

Van Gennup, Arnold, 91–92
verbal abuse, 37

Walumbwa, F. O., 23–24
wellness retreats, 69
Werner, O., 17
Wilson, S., 7
Witt, P., 36
Witten, H., 14
Woods-Jaeger, B., 15
Working on Womanhood program,
34–35

youth advisory boards, 60–61, 62
youth executive boards (e-board), 62
Youth Guidance programs (Chicago),
34–35
youth practitioners
description, 53
disappointments in/poor reputations
of, 31, 53
elements in making curriculum
choices, 55
skill level shortcomings, 53
traits for success, 54
values/skills/talents requirements,
56–57